# OWN YOUR VOICE

### 8 Emotional Habits That Empower Women to Be Seen, Heard, and Fearless

## MARGO TIRADO MA, LCPC

Chingona Media

# CONTENTS

**Publisher's Cataloging-in-Publication Data**
Tirado, Margo M. 1965—.
Own Your Voice: 8 Habits That Empower Women to Be Seen, Heard, and Fearless / Margo Tirado
p.____ cm.____
ISBN: 978-1-947834-63-7 (Pbk.) | ISBN: 978-1-947834-64-4 (Ebook)
1. Women's Issues. 2. Psychology. 3. Self-Help. I. Title.
158'.1 | LCCN: 2022902769

Published by Chingona Media
PO Box 242, Western Springs, Illinois 60558
www.chingona-media.com

Cover Design by Lauren Faulkenberry
Cover Illustrations by JoyCrew

*To Frank,*

*You are my steady love,*
*my heart,*
*my soul,*
*my breath,*
*the best thing that ever happened to me.*

*I love you more than tacos!*

# PRAISE FOR OWN YOUR VOICE

Oh, this book!!! … So very wise and true and powerful and necessary. Margo's wisdom and voice offer a powerful and essential conversation for every woman. With great strength and care, Margo helps us unpack the roadblocks, lies, and false narratives that keep us from owning our voice. She calls out the negative influences that hinder us as women and unleashes us to lead in powerful, vivid, and magnificent ways. Her personal stories provide an accessible space to enter this dialogue on leadership and power, and her generous heart leads us to new sources of strength and vision. In short, Margo brings it on!

—REV. TRACEY BIANCHI, PASTOR, AUTHOR OF *TRUE YOU*, AND PROFESSOR AT THE CENTER FOR WOMEN IN LEADERSHIP AT NORTHERN SEMINARY

This book will teach you how to be "chingona"—that is, to be powerful, fierce and unapologetically own who you are.

—JOY DONNELL, PRODUCER, ACTIVIST, AND AUTHOR OF *BEYOND BRAND*

In *Own Your Voice*, Margo Tirado brilliantly lays out 8 emotional habits that provide a clear path toward becoming the strongest version of yourself. An eye-opening read from a talented storyteller, Tirado's passion for empowering women is heard loud and clear throughout the book. This is a must read for all women because our voices need to be heard.

—JODI BONDI NORGAARD, FOUNDER GO! GO! SPORTS GIRLS AND AUTHOR OF *MORE THAN A DOLL: HOW CREATING A NEW BRAND OF DOLLS TURNED INTO A FIGHT TO END GENDER STEREOTYPES*

Reading Margo Tirado's words…was an invitation to a homecoming to my Authentic Self. It was inspiring and empowering. I felt seen and heard by Margo as I read of experiences…that had her silencing her voice. I, like many women, have done the same.

She provides very specific, easy-to-grasp tools for turning that silencing around and claiming our feminine authority. She does this by reminding us if you don't know and believe in yourself, others will see you in the same way. I especially loved the reminder, "When you walk into a room, you bring all of the beliefs you have about yourself with you." That was extremely enlightening! Thank you, Margo for helping women become comfortable with being visible!

—CATHERINE DEMONTE,
PSYCHOTHERAPIST AND COACH AND
AUTHOR OF *BEEP! BEEP! GET OUT OF
MY WAY! SEVEN TOOLS FOR POWERFUL
CREATION*

An inspirational, motivating, and highly practical guide to owning your power and stepping into leadership. Filled with concrete insights, Tirado's book outlines strategic steps women can take to begin to cultivate larger-scale influence. She speaks to needs that are common to most women I know and that resonate deeply with my own soul. This is an incredibly helpful…guidebook I will refer to again and again.

—KAREN KINNEY, AUTHOR OF
*DOORWAYS TO TRANSFORMATION:
EVERYDAY WISDOM FOR THE CREATIVE
SOUL*

Many women live a lifetime trying to find their voice and working to own the space we inhabit in the world. Margo Tirado not only walks with us on the journey of finding our voice but of amplifying it for the good of ourselves and the world. She asks hard questions that can help us heal, all while getting stronger. This is a must-read for any woman trying to become emotionally healthy and self-confident in who she is created to be!

—ANITA LUSTREA, AUTHOR OF *WHAT
WOMEN TELL ME, SHADES OF MERCY*,
AND *TENDING THE SOUL,* AND HOST OF
THE *FAITH CONVERSATIONS* PODCAST

Margo has written a brilliant book that should be in the hands of every woman. She uses her experience as a psychotherapist, powerful story-telling, and a step-by-step description of how to step into leadership and make your mark in the world!

—BRIAN KURBJEWEIT, BEST-SELLING AUTHOR OF *THE LEADERSHIP SPACE*

This book is a must-read for any woman looking to be more visible, and step into her power. We desperately need more and bolder women's voices in the world so Margo's book couldn't come at a better time. Building resilience, inner confidence and lowering your tolerance to crap sometimes seems like a life-long path of unlearning who we have been thought to be. This book gives you some powerful tools to find the strength to speak up, by addressing often overlooked emotional habits that truly make a difference!

—MURIELLE MARIE, BUSINESS & CAREER COACH FOR CREATIVES AND ENTREPRENEURS

Change in this world is dependent on more powerful, paradigm-shifting women raising their voices and demanding a change in the conversation. And Margo Tirado is teaching us to do just that. If you've ever felt small, voiceless, even weak and silenced, Margo delivers important lessons, tools, and encouragement that will help all of us "own our voices" and affect much-needed change on an individual and worldwide level.

—AMANDA BERLIN, *EMPOWERED PUBLICITY* PODCAST

Own your voice! Master the fear that seeks to master you! In the hands of some, those phrases are clichés, but Margo Tirado's wisdom gets underneath slogans and soundbites to introduce you to the person you have longed to meet: yourself. Tirado's stories will make you wince in recognition and squirm in that kind of "I've done that too!" awareness before depositing you into a reflective space where real self-analysis and change can occur. Filled with thoughtful exercises and writing prompts, this book is a cross between a how-to guide and a long conversation with a great friend. Be prepared though: you won't end this book in the same way you started it.

—REV. DR. LAURA SUMNER TRUAX,
AUTHOR OF *LOVE LET GO* AND
*UNDONE*, AND SENIOR MINISTER OF
LASALLE STREET CHURCH IN CHICAGO,
ILLINOIS

This book is genius! Reading her book was like listening to a series of TED talks—she uses her personal stories to deliver the content with powerful metaphors that make these habits easy to understand and apply immediately. Margo is a mentor and a teacher all wrapped into one.

—J. ANTONIO, AUTHOR OF *ALWAYS
SAY HI*

# FOREWORD
TABBY BIDDLE

There are so many women today who are searching for their voice—their true, authentic voice. We women want access to this voice because we know deep inside that it is the pathway to our self-fulfillment, full self-expression and joy, and the pathway to our greater leadership, influence, and power. We are tired of people-pleasing, putting other people's needs and voices above our own, and diminishing ourselves in the face of others.

We have spent centuries being told we "are less than," "are not worthy," "don't matter," and other things much worse. The oppression of women and girls and the silencing of our voices is a global phenomenon. From India to Saudi Arabia, China, and the United States, we are suffering under a patriarchal culture that devalues women.

As a women's leadership coach, gender equity advocate, and writer focusing on women, leadership and power, I have seen firsthand and close-up the challenges women face when it comes to finding their voices. I, too, have encountered many of these same challenges.

I first met Margo Tirado seven years ago when she enrolled in my "Write Your Book" course for female changemakers and emerging feminine leaders. Margo was a licensed clinical professional counselor with a Master's Degree in Clinical Psychology from Wheaton College. She was seeing clients one-on-one and now had a desire to serve more women.

In 2017, Margo presented at TEDx Grant Park in Chicago on "How to Quiet a Shame-Producing Toxic Voice." She not only aced it on stage—fully owning *her* voice, her expertise, and her feminine authority—she nailed the flamenco dance she wove into her TEDx talk. She was a great inspiration.

After Margo gave her TEDx talk, she was in high demand. She was being invited as an expert speaker on gender-specific therapy at conferences, workshops, radio, and podcast interviews. She was also being invited to speak at faith-based organizations to share her thoughts about the absence of women in leadership and how to close that gap.

As Margo spoke more, her platform grew, and the urgency of her message became more apparent.

In this book that you now hold in your hands, Margo brings her 30 years of experience as a psychotherapist—as well as the wisdom, depth, and richness of her own personal journey— to support you in overcoming long-held habitual emotional patterns and limiting beliefs to finally own and use your voice in the way that you have longed to do.

Margo will help you speak up, set boundaries, let go of

perfectionism, take more risks, lower your tolerance for crap, and invest more in liking yourself instead of in being likable.

While the work ahead may feel challenging, when you do it, it will provide you with lifelong benefits. These personal benefits will have a ripple effect on your family, your friends, your colleagues, your community, your country, and our world.

This work matters. You matter. Your voice matters. You have the opportunity to right the wrongs inflicted on women who came before you and blaze a path ahead for future generations of women.

Over the years I've known Margo, I've had the great pleasure of watching her build her leadership platform and amplify her voice to make a positive difference in the world. I find it thrilling to see her use her expertise in researching and developing gender-specific therapeutic insights that empower women to appreciate and honor the power of their voices. She is a much-needed resource in our world.

Margo has told me that she has the goal to empower a million women in her lifetime. Through her psychotherapy practice, public speaking, article writing, workshops, retreats, and radio and podcast interviews, I'd say she is well on her way to meeting this goal. With this book, I believe she will surpass it.

This is the kind of book that you'll want to share with your friends, colleagues, and family—and frankly, any woman you know who is struggling with the common challenge of owning her voice and fully stepping into who she came here to be.

As Margo says in the following pages, "When a woman

has a strong voice, she is able to amplify her values, own her perspective, and govern the trajectory of her future."

It is with deep love, encouragement, and excitement that I leave you now to embark on this journey with Margo. You are in great hands. Margo will walk with you every step of the way so that you can govern the trajectory of your future.

And so it is.

Tabby Biddle
Women's Leadership Coach and Gender Equity Advocate
Author of *Find Your Voice: A Woman's Call to Action*

January, 2022
Santa Monica, California

# INTRODUCTION

When I was in my early forties, I decided to hire a woman named Paula as my personal trainer. I needed help building a stronger body and gaining more control over my health. I expected to have difficulty with the physical demands of the workout since I had not been in the habit of exercising for a while. I'll never forget how challenging training was. On the first day of training, Paula pushed me hard, determined to help me build muscle strength. I ran laps, balanced kettle balls, attempted bicep curls (to no avail), and more. At times, I felt nauseated and thought I might pass out. Midway through the workout, Paula told me to hit the ground and do twenty full-body push-ups. When she wasn't looking, I gave her the stink-eye and then begrudgingly got on my hands and knees in preparation. After the first push-up, my muscles began to spasm and shake. After the second push-up, my body conceded defeat, my arms went limp, and suddenly I was lying face-first on the ground.

"I can't do it, Paula. I don't have the strength!" I whimpered. Of course, this made sense—I was weak because I hadn't worked at building muscle strength for quite a while.

A few days later, I was providing counseling sessions to several women. Each of these women had her own distinctive story and personality, but all of them were struggling with similar experiences. They felt stuck. They felt weak. They told me how tired they were of feeling like their voice didn't matter. They'd had enough of feeling "less than" and "not good enough." They were tired of people-pleasing and tolerating crap. They wanted more self-fulfillment, influence, and power. They wanted to know how to turn up the volume on their voices and be heard so they could change the things that mattered to them. They wanted to feel more empowered. They wanted to *be* more empowered!

Their words were a theme I had heard from virtually every woman I have worked with in the last thirty years as a psychotherapist and coach. I kept thinking about their words as I left the office and drove to the gym. Then a thought occurred to me. **Our emotional habits are a lot like muscles: what we practice grows stronger. Just as working out can build stronger muscles, working on emotional strength can build a powerful voice.** I needed to figure out how I could teach women the emotional strength that would lead to having a powerful voice. Once a woman had a powerful voice, she could change the things that mattered to her.

For the next several years, I began to study and document the emotional habits that empower women, knowing that these habits were the key that would unlock the door to helping women have stronger voices. I knew if I could open this door, I could do more than help women get unstuck and strengthen their resolve to address their current personal struggles. I could empower them for a lifetime. Powerful emotional habits strengthen a woman's voice and consequently, strengthen her ability to change the things that matter to her.

To accomplish this task, I gathered the wisdom of thousands of women that I'd gained through my profession. Bringing together their collective stories—as well as my own —I could understand the specific challenges women face when they set out to have a bigger voice in the world. I wanted to help women remove any self-doubt that might keep them from possessing self-confidence, influence, and power. I used my training as a psychotherapist to create gender-specific insights so that I could teach women new patterns of thinking. For the next ten years, I focused on researching, describing, and teaching women the emotional habits that are the building blocks of a powerful voice.

**When a woman owns her voice, she becomes clear about what she values, what she stands for, and how to move her beliefs into action.** The power of her voice flows from the confidence that comes from unapologetically owning who she is.

Over time, as I taught these emotional habits, I noticed specific changes in how my clients behaved:

- Women began to speak up about the issues that mattered to them.

- Women were lowering their tolerance for crap. They were setting boundaries, asserting their decision-making power, and breaking free from people-pleasing habits.
- Women were stepping into leadership. They were taking up space with their thoughts, ideas, and perspectives. They were stepping out of the shadows and making themselves seen and heard. They were exuding confidence, power, and authority.
- Women were no longer concerned about failing. Instead, they were getting out of their comfort zones, taking more risks, and pursuing bigger opportunities. They were tapping into their inner resources to manage the fear that came from doing so.
- Women were becoming more self-accepting. They were no longer putting pressure on themselves to be perfect or never make mistakes. Instead, they were embracing the power of being "good enough" and living more authentically.
- Women were boldly and confidently sharing their perspectives on both small and larger platforms, firmly believing that what they had to say mattered. With determination, they were pursuing the vision of what they wanted to accomplish.

**These emotional habits empowered women to own their voices.** They helped women claim their inherent power. Little habits became big habits as women flexed these new emotional muscles.

After teaching these habits in my private practice, I started teaching them on larger platforms: retreats, podcasts, conferences, leadership training, webinars, radio, and so on. In 2017, I gave a TEDx talk in Grant Park Chicago on the topic. I have been teaching women across the country how to build these habits into their lives so they can unleash the power of their voices. This book is the accumulation of those insights.

Here is a preview of this book.

- With the exception of Chapter One, "The Habit of Owning Your Voice: How to Build Powerful Emotional Habits into your Life," each chapter was designed to be read independently of the other. Once you've read the first chapter, read the chapters that best describe where you need the most support and are most relevant to you at this moment in time. We are all at different stages in our growth, and it's okay to focus on where you need the most support.

- I have included dozens of coaching tools throughout the book that are designed to help you build strong habits in your life. These coaching tools include writing prompts and reflection questions designed to help you immediately begin applying the book's insights to your unique situation. I recommend having a pen and journal handy so you will have a place to write down your thoughts and reactions to the writing prompts in this book.

- While I hope you will take the time to read the whole book, I understand that life is busy and demanding. Sometimes we need to skim the content in between work and family obligations. I get that. So I have summarized each chapter for you. You can find these summaries at the end of each chapter in the section called "In a Nutshell."

- This is the kind of book you might want to discuss with coworkers and friends. With that in mind, I have added several conversation starters at the end of each chapter that will help spark some hearty and much-needed discussions.

- I wrote this book specifically for women to empower women. It is my way to help level the playing field. However, men and gender-nonconforming people will also relate to the habits discussed in this book. In my practice, though, I have found that, by and large, these concepts will be more relatable to women. For this reason, I have used feminine pronouns as the "neutral" pronouns in the book.

- I have included the stories of clients. All of their names and identifying details have been changed to protect their privacy.

For better or worse, our emotional habits have the power to shape the relationship we have with ourselves and others.

We each have the power to build the emotional habits that can help us influence the things that matter most to us, empower us, and help us find self-fulfillment.

It's time to release the most powerful force in the world...you!

# CHAPTER 1
# THE HABIT OF OWNING YOUR VOICE

## HOW TO BUILD POWERFUL EMOTIONAL HABITS INTO YOUR LIFE

I n 1987, when I was twenty-two years old, I was sitting inside our adobe-style apartment when my sister Bertha walked in with the mail. In her hand was a massive envelope from Wheaton College, a prestigious university in Illinois. The envelope held my acceptance into their graduate school for my master's degree in psychology, and I was ecstatic. I felt like this small-town New Mexican girl had just accomplished the impossible. I had fantasized about being a counselor ever since I was a little girl. To this day, I have fond memories of me with my sisters, playing make-believe: we would pretend to be waitresses and teachers, but my favorite role was pretending I was a counselor.

After celebrating my good news with my sister, I jumped into my white Ford pickup and made my way to my grandpa's home in Santa Fe. He was one of the most important people in my life, and I couldn't wait to tell him about Wheaton. I burst into his casita, spilling over with pride and excitement, and shared the news. I was unprepared for his response.

Grandpa said he was disappointed in me. He couldn't believe I would consider leaving my family and homeland to pursue higher education. He told me that instead, I should go to the local university, where I could get the same education. He reasoned that doing so would be more cost-effective and would not require I leave my family behind or live alone in a land he had no knowledge of. Upset with me, he said he could not comprehend why I would ever want to leave my family.

Grandpa could not understand why a woman would leave her home, family, and culture to pursue higher education. This was 1987 and, as a woman of color, I was already considered highly accomplished: I had both a high school education and a college degree. From his perspective, I had already broken the glass ceiling. At that time, there weren't many examples of Latina women with graduate degrees, much less ones who had left their families to earn them.[1]

I understood his position. Even though I experienced a lot of heartache and abuse within my nuclear family, I had a large, loving extended family that I cared for deeply, and I loved my nuclear family as well. I didn't want to leave them. I was raised in a large Catholic family with seven children. Beyond my nuclear family, I had eight maternal aunts (all of whom I was close to), several uncles, dozens of cousins, and many nieces and nephews. We all lived within sixty miles of each other. I knew that leaving for school would also mean leaving behind the comfort of my friends, the safety net of my large family, and the familiarity of my culture. I felt afraid to leave behind the known and venture into the unknown. I didn't know what to expect once I left our town behind, and I had no friends or family who would be waiting to greet me when I arrived in my new home-away-from-home. I would have to rely on a new and unknown group of supporters.

I left Grandpa's house with a knot in my stomach, wrestling with my thoughts. As I drove home, the desert land surrounding the highway suddenly seemed more desolate and bleaker.

Grandpa's disapproval caught me off guard. That moment was the first and only time I'd ever felt his disappointment, and it was awful. He was the most influential person in my life. Grandpa's unconditional love had laid the foundation for my inner strength. When he voiced his disapproval of my educational plans, I felt pulled between yearning for his approval and pursuing my most important dream.

But I didn't give up. I began taking weekly trips to see Grandpa, with the hopes of eventually gaining his approval. More importantly, I wanted the "bendición," which is a blessing one receives from an older family member or elder, given on special occasions and always before one traveled. I needed to know I would receive my grandfather's bendición if I chose to leave my family and pursue graduate school far away. During our visits, I shared every reason I could come up with for why attending Wheaton was a grand opportunity, and then he shared every worry he had about me leaving. He would not budge on his perspective, while I could not imagine giving up this opportunity.

Week after week I struggled with my decision. I did not

like the idea of upsetting my grandpa, but I knew if I declined Wheaton's offer, I would regret the decision. Adding to this pressure, I was young, naïve, and inexperienced with the world. I was already in debt with undergraduate loans, and I had $275 in my bank account. I had only flown on an airplane once in my entire life. I remember studying a map and counting the number of states between Illinois and New Mexico, taking note of the distance between the school and my family. In short, I was really scared.

I was also aware of the rules assigned to me by my patriarchal Latino Catholic culture, a culture that declared my greatest accomplishment would be to get married, have kids, and serve my family. Seeking a higher education, being a successful professional, making good money, and seeking national opportunities was not the cultural norm for the women of my culture and my generation. Ambition was frowned upon. Family-centered goals were applauded.

One day, I sat in my pickup and asked myself, "What is the underlying motivation keeping me from choosing to leave New Mexico to go to graduate school?" After a bit of reflection, it became clearer to me that I was motivated by a desire to please others. I wanted approval from my grandpa and my Latino family in general. I was also motivated by the praise that came with being a more traditional Latina woman who put family over career.

What I discovered was that these motivations were the source of two deeply ingrained emotional habits: the habit of people-pleasing and the habit of doing what was expected of me. For me, these emotional habits were on autopilot and ultimately caused me to give away the power to make this decision. I still hadn't learned how to own my voice and make decisions that were based on my perspective and who I was at the core. If I was going to live without limits, I would need to stop driving on autopilot and become more aware of why I was driving from point A to point B.

Suddenly, I became more aware of how my emotional habits were driving me. **An emotional habit is a pattern of thinking or behaving that is on autopilot.** We all have emotional habits that we repeat over and over again without any thought, often without realizing their influence over how we make decisions, how we view ourselves, and the anatomy of our lives.

I needed to shift gears, break the habit of people-pleasing, and instead assert my perspective and accept the disapproval that might result from doing so. I needed to break the habit of trying to fit into any preconceived ideas about what it meant to be a Latina woman and instead be my true self. My true self was both traditional and modern. I embraced many of the traditional aspects of the Latin culture, but I believed in a more modern Latina woman who could be both family-oriented and professionally successful. Instead of giving away my decision-making power, I needed to own it and all the responsibility that came with it. I could not give this decision to Grandpa or anybody else in my life.

All too soon, Wheaton's deadline arrived, and it was time to decide whether to go. Fortunately, I had shifted out of autopilot and was entirely aware of where my inner voice was leading me. I knew who I was and therefore I knew what I needed to do. I took a deep breath and sent my acceptance letter to Wheaton College. I was going to travel beyond familiar territory even though I was unsure of what would be on the other side.

My grandfather was disappointed with my decision, but eventually, he did give me the bendición. The amusing part of this story is the reason he eventually chose to do so. At one point in my conversation with him, I happened to mention that Frank, my boyfriend at the time, would also be living near Wheaton College. Living closer to each other would allow Frank and me the opportunity to determine whether we would marry. The notion of marriage thrilled my very Catholic grandpa, who adored my very Catholic boyfriend.

I received my grandfather's blessing and went to graduate school. Frank and I did eventually get married. So, you could say I had my wedding cake and got to eat it too. Just as important, I began to learn new emotional habits that would empower me for the rest of my life. Instead of pleasing others and doing what was expected of me, I began to own my voice and use it to clear a new path for not only myself but also for my nieces and their future daughters— creating a world where ambitious family-centered women were the new normal.

The episode between my grandfather and me reveals how long-standing emotional habits can impede us from owning our voices, especially when others are questioning our perspective. It also demonstrates how our culture and relationships can impact the emotional habits we form. Emotional habits form for all sorts of reasons. Throughout this book, we will explore how they develop. We will also learn how to become aware of how habits shape our lives and voice and how to cultivate the emotional habits that will make us stronger.

In this chapter, I will reveal a three-step process to help cultivate healthy emotional habits that will help you own your voice and live without limits. You can use this three-step process to develop every habit mentioned in this book. Here is an overview of the process.

**1. Be aware of your emotional habits.** Awareness is power. The more you can name, describe, and understand the impact of your emotional habits, the more you will be able to discern if your habits are empowering you or holding you back.

**2. Shift gears and move out of autopilot.** Instead of repeating the same habits over and over, you can change how you think, behave, and react. This change lays the foundation for establishing new emotional habits.

**3. What you practice grows stronger.** This step involves building new emotional habits into your daily life until they are strong and automatic. When you create new habits, your brain changes with you. When you practice new behaviors, you are also creating new neural pathways that help you repeat new habits with more ease.

Your voice is the most valuable resource you own. When a woman has a strong voice, she can amplify her values, own her perspective, and govern the trajectory of her future. Before describing the three-step process of cultivating healthy emotional habits, let's learn more about how strong emotional habits and owning your voice are interconnected.

## YOUR EMOTIONAL HABITS AND YOUR VOICE WORK IN TANDEM

As you learned earlier in this chapter, emotional habits are a pattern of thoughts and behaviors on autopilot. These habits lay the foundation for a lot of what happens in our lives. Emotional habits shape our relationships, our confidence, how people relate to us, our job status, how we make decisions, the opportunities we pursue, and so much more!

From a clinical perspective, emotional habits determine two big things:

First, emotional habits determine whether you are living an empowered life. Living an empowered life means having the ability to influence the things that matter most to you.

Second, emotional habits determine whether you have a powerful voice. **Your voice is the authentic expression of your values, your perspective, and who you are at the core.** When a woman has a strong voice, she better understands what she values, what she stands for, and how to move her beliefs into action.

In my role as a psychotherapist, I have been teaching women how to build powerful emotional habits into their lives for over thirty years. Repeatedly, I have witnessed how my clients' lives began to change when they became aware of the emotional patterns that were keeping them from asserting their perspective and from living with more confidence. I wait in anticipation between sessions, knowing that when I see them again in session, their faces will light up as they tell stories of how good it feels to practice new habits such as speaking up, setting boundaries, lowering their tolerance for crap, letting go of perfectionism, and investing more in liking themselves instead of in being likable.

Your emotional habits work in tandem with your voice— they can either strengthen the innate power of your voice or diminish it. That's why building strong emotional habits is the key to being able to confidently express your voice.

## STEP ONE: BE AWARE OF YOUR EMOTIONAL HABITS

We are unaware of many of our habits. We repeat our habits over and over again, often without much thought. The first step towards building new or empowering habits is to become aware of the thoughts and behaviors you are repeating right now. You must bring your emotional habits into view so that you can notice how they are impacting your life. Then you can decide whether it's necessary to change them.

Here, I will show you how to become more aware of your emotional habits by naming them, describing them, and understanding their impact on your life. I will provide a series of four powerful questions that will gently lead you towards understanding your emotional habits and whether the habits are working for or against you. I will also share stories from my life and the life of my clients that demonstrate the impact emotional habits can have on self-confidence, relationships, and self-fulfillment.

When we brush our teeth, it doesn't take much thought. In fact, when I brush my teeth I can step into my closet, pick out clothing for the day, place the outfit on my bed, return to the bathroom sink, and spit, wash, and rinse. The habit of brushing my teeth is such an established pattern that I can do it without thinking. I brush my teeth on autopilot. We repeat our emotional habits in the same way we brush our teeth—on autopilot and without much thought. We repeat our emotional habits daily, and frequently with little awareness.

My long history of being a people-pleaser is a good example of how we automatically repeat the same thoughts and behaviors without realizing the impact these habits are having on our lives. When I was a child, my family home was a volatile environment that often left me feeling helpless. I had a brother who was particularly aggressive. As a way of adapting and protecting myself from him, I figured out how to appease him. Appeasing him meant taking care of him: I cooked his meals, for example, and engaged in similar behaviors that "pleased" him. So long as I appeased him, the less likely I was to fall prey to his verbal and physical aggression. Thus, as a young girl, my people-pleasing habits served an important self-protective function. However, I brought my self-sabotaging people-pleasing habits into adulthood—for example, setting aside my own needs to help others, chronically taking care of people at the expense of my own mental health, being overly responsive to the requests of others, and so on. And just like brushing my teeth, I practiced my people-pleasing habit regularly and without much awareness of how it was shaping my adult relationships and identity.

Eventually, I was able to break free from the habit of people-pleasing. One day I noticed how exhausted I was following a visit with my family. I realized the mental exhaustion was stemming from a tendency to chronically take care of my family and do things that would ensure their happiness. As a result, when I was with them, I rarely chose to do the things that would energize me or make me happy. This habit had nothing to do with my family's expectations of me and everything to do with the expectations I had placed on myself. So I decided it was time to change how I was behaving and thinking. To change my habit, I would need to become more conscious of these patterns. To do so, I started by asking myself the same four "Habit Questions" that I ask my clients when we are working on cultivating new habits.

Below are the four Habit Questions. I also included my own answers. I used the following questions to understand the impact people-pleasing was having on my life so I could change this pattern.

*Four Habit Questions*

1. Describe and name a negative habit you are repeating in your life. Remember, an emotional habit is a pattern of thinking or behaving that is on autopilot.

My answer: My negative habit is people-pleasing. I tend to automatically zoom in on other people's needs and desires and then make myself responsible for them; this happens not just in my relationship with my family but in many of my relationships.

2. What is motivating this habit?

My answer: My behaviors are motivated by a desire to feel valued by others. However, the habit has also perpetuated the belief that if I were to stop catering to the needs of others, I will be less valuable. Part of my identity has been defined by being the person who takes care of others. Instead of being valued for taking care of others, I want to be valued just for being me.

3. How is this emotional habit impacting your life? Is it helping you or preventing you from living a more empowered life? Living an empowered life means being able to influence the things that matter most to you.

My answer: The habit of people-pleasing is preventing me from influencing the things that matter to me because it prevents me from expressing my opinion. I tend to be hyper-focused on what is important to others and omit my own perspective. This pattern perpetuates the belief of myself that my view is unimportant.

4. Will changing this habit help you cultivate a more powerful voice? Your voice is the authentic expression

of your values, perspective, and who you are at the core.

My answer: Yes, because the habit of people-pleasing is keeping me from expressing my needs. I am so focused on responding to the desires of others, I often have no idea what I need, and I have an even harder time vocalizing it. Instead of speaking up, I am more likely to be silent and agreeable. I want to find a better balance and find ways to take care of others and myself.

As you can see, these questions helped me deepen my awareness of how the habit of people-pleasing was shaping my life. Suddenly, I could see that the habit that protected me as a young girl was not protecting me as an adult. It was harming my ability to pay attention to what I needed, and it was preventing me from saying no to mentally exhausting situations. These questions helped me understand what was motivating me to repeat these patterns. I finally understood that people-pleasing was keeping me from feeling loved for who I am instead of valued for what I give to others. This understanding was empowering.

Don't let your emotional habits fly under your radar and out of your awareness, even your positive ones! Doing so will cause you to repeat them without any thought and without any understanding of how your habits are shaping your life. Instead, take charge of your habits—good and bad—by becoming more conscious of them.

Take a look at the following negative emotional habits and

ask yourself if any of them seem familiar.

- Having a high tolerance for crap instead of setting self-protective boundaries
- Ignoring your needs instead of listening to your voice and asking for what you want
- Being critical of yourself instead of accepting all of who you are, including your imperfections
- Giving your power away instead of owning your authority
- Making yourself small instead of making sure you are heard and seen
- Investing in being likable instead of investing in knowing and being your authentic self
- Dismissing your feelings instead of acknowledging that how you feel matters
- Avoiding risks instead of getting out of your comfort zone and pursuing greater opportunities
- Giving others the power to make decisions for you instead of owning the power to make those decisions for yourself

**Self-awareness is power!** When you become even a little more aware of the emotional habits in your life, you become more empowered.

If one or more of the negative emotional habits on the list above are familiar to you, use the four Habit Questions to discern whether they are working for or against you. I provided my personal answers earlier, using my people-pleasing tendencies as an example. Use the following coaching questions to become more conscious of your emotional habits. If it helps, write down your answers in a journal.

*A Coaching Moment:*
*The Four Habit Questions*

1. Describe and name a negative emotional habit that you are repeating in your life. You can choose from the list above or choose a different one. Recall that a habit is a pattern of thinking or behaving on autopilot.

2. What is motivating this emotional habit?

3. How is this emotional habit impacting your life? Is it helping you or preventing you from living a more empowered life? Remember, living an empowered life means having the ability to influence the things that matter most to you.

4. Will changing this emotional habit help you cultivate a more powerful voice? Your voice is the authentic expression of your values, perspective, and who you are at the core.

## STEP TWO: SHIFT GEARS AND MOVE OUT OF AUTOPILOT

When we build more awareness around our emotional habits by discovering how to name them, describe them, and understand their impact on our lives, we can then take the next step towards changing them. That next step is shifting gears and moving our emotional habits out of autopilot. When we shift how we think, behave, and react, our lives and relationships will shift as well.

Many airplanes are built to fly on autopilot if necessary. Despite the autopilot feature, every pilot knows how to fly a plane manually. Now, imagine you are a pilot who has decided to disengage the autopilot system and fly manually instead. This shift means that every decision you make in the cockpit will need to be intentional. **That's how you change emotional habits as well—you shift gears, move out of autopilot, and choose to operate with intention.** The opposite of living on autopilot is living intentionally.

Developing new emotional habits requires consciously taking control of the plane and flying with more awareness. **Instead of thinking and behaving on autopilot, be deliberate about choosing the thoughts and actions that will empower you.** Doing so will mean you will need to try new ways of behaving. Trying new behaviors will push you out of your comfort zone, but the positive outcomes will be incredibly rewarding.

I worked with an inspiring client named Gabriela (not her real name) who had recently become aware she was in the habit of giving her decision-making power away by deferring to her strong-willed husband's choices. For example, she acquiesced to his decision to buy an eighty-five-inch TV for his man cave even though their finances were strained. She conceded to having her critical mother-in-law join them for family dinner every Sunday. She gave in when he insisted on seeing her receipts for household expenses. Gabriela was ready to change the way she was thinking and reacting so that she could move her life patterns out of autopilot.

Gabriela was a social worker who was fully capable of making effective choices, but over time she got into the habit of withholding her perspective, not speaking up, avoiding conflict, and ultimately deferring decisions to her husband, Pedro. Throughout their ten-year marriage, Pedro constantly challenged Gabriela's perspective in all matters. He belittled her decisions until she backed down. Pedro aggressively defended his point of view and argued with Gabriela until she inevitably caved. Over time, Gabriela grew weary of the conflict, debates, and the feeling of being criticized by Pedro when she tried to stand her ground and share her perspective. Craving harmony and the absence of conflict, Gabriela got into the habit of automatically letting Pedro make the decisions in the relationship, thus giving her decision-making power to Pedro. Gabriela also brought this habit into her professional life.

One day in session, Gabriela shared that she had recently remained silent in a conversation with Pedro regarding a decision to invite two friends over for dinner. She felt uncomfortable spending time with this couple because they had a history of making comments about her weight and mocking cultures that were different from their own. Instead of speaking up and facing the tension that would come from doing so, she'd said nothing. Gabriela told me she was tired of feeling invisible and powerless and was ready to change. She wanted to take control and have a conversation with Pedro about choosing friends who were more inclusive and accepting. She wanted her perspective to be included in their decision-making.

In a previous session, Gabriela had already processed the four Habit Questions that I ask my clients when we are working on cultivating new emotional habits. Because of this earlier work, Gabriela was already aware of the habit she wanted to change—the habit of giving away the power to make decisions. She was able to describe it (withholding her perspective, not speaking up, avoiding conflict, deferring decisions to others), and she understood the impact it was having on her life (making her feel invisible and powerless).

So, I asked her two coaching questions that would help her shift gears, take back control, and try a new way of thinking. Here are the two questions I asked her along with a paraphrase of her answers:

1. Describe a moment in your life when you deferred decisions to someone else, instead of owning the power to make the decision for yourself.

Gabriela: Pedro and I decided to invite friends over for dinner. As we began to discuss our options, Pedro decided he wanted to invite a couple from his bowling league. I am not fond of the couple Pedro chose. In the past, they have commented on the amount of weight I've gained. Fat jokes and culturally insensitive comments are common with this couple. When I objected, Pedro cut me off and insisted that this was the couple he wanted to invite. I do not want to spend time with this couple. Their comments are offensive, and they make me uncomfortable. However, instead of speaking up and setting boundaries, I gave in.

I now realize that, when I remain silent, I am giving all the decision-making power to Pedro. When Pedro and I disagree, as soon as I sense he is frustrated with my perspective, I back down because I dislike the feeling of being challenged. Typically, I don't initiate discussions regarding matters that are important to me. As a result, Pedro makes most of the decisions in our marriage.

2. If you could shift gears and own your decision-making power instead of automatically giving it away, what would you do differently? Describe at least three ways you would like to shift your thoughts or behaviors.

Gabriela:

I can remind myself that what I have to say matters.

I can speak up even if it means creating tension between Pedro and me.

I can manage the discomfort of being challenged and remind myself that it's okay to create tension to protect something I value.

I can set boundaries and insist my perspective be

included. If Pedro tries to invite this couple to our home without my consent, I will make it clear I object. I will hold my ground until my views are included.

I will refuse to be there if this couple is present. I will not allow him to bully me. Instead, I will defend my decision to spend time with people I feel at ease with and who are more culturally sensitive.

As Gabriela reflected on her responses, she saw clearly what she needed to do. She left my office with a spirit of hope, clarity, and a determination to take back her power. The following week, Gabriela returned to the office with a huge grin on her face. She had initiated a conversation with Pedro regarding whom she wanted them to spend time with as a couple. After sharing her concerns, Pedro began to dismiss her perspective and argue about the merits of the couple. Throughout their two-hour conversation, Gabriela held her ground, took deep breaths when needed, reminded herself that the conflict had a purpose, and did not retreat. In the end, Pedro understood Gabriela's perspective and agreed to invite a couple they both liked.

Gabriela seemed a foot taller as she sat in front of me telling her story. She told me it felt great finding her voice and using it! She was experiencing what I have seen thousands of women experience when they begin to develop empowering emotional habits:

- They are more confident and bolder.
- They embody the belief that what they have to say

matters.
- They have healthier relationships with themselves and others.
- They establish better boundaries.
- They turn up the volume of their voice in every area of their life.

When we become aware of our emotional habits that are on autopilot and shift towards those that empower us, we can reshape the anatomy of our lives. We can access our innate power to change our circumstances. When you are ready to take back control from autopilot, these coaching questions will help you accomplish that goal.

*A Coaching Moment:*
*Three Questions to Shift Gears*
*and Take Back Control*

1. Name the emotional habit you want to change.

2. Describe a moment in your life when you exhibited this habit.

3. If you could take back control from autopilot and change this habit, what would you want to do differently next time? Describe at least three ways you would like to shift your thoughts or behaviors.

Just like Gabriela, we each have the power to shift our circumstances when we shift our emotional habits. Don't repeat the same patterns that are keeping you from having a strong voice. Instead, be acutely aware of how your emotional habits are shaping your life. Name them, describe them, and understand their impact on your life. Then take back control from autopilot and develop new, more empowering habits. Soon, little habits will become big habits.

## STEP THREE: WHAT WE PRACTICE GROWS STRONGER

If you asked me to get down on the floor and do twenty full-body push-ups, I could probably manage to complete two, but only with a lot of effort and huffing and puffing. If, however, every morning after drinking my first cup of coffee I pulled out my yoga mat, got on the floor, and committed to working on push-ups, over time I could easily complete twenty. **Our emotional habits are a lot like muscles: what we practice grows stronger.** The key to developing strong habits is to routinely develop the emotional muscles that will help you build confidence and your voice.

When we engage in well-established habits, we do not use the thinking centers of our brain, but instead operate on autopilot. This happens because the behaviors we repeat over and over create neural connections in our brain, developing deeply ingrained pathways. As we repeat these actions, the neural connections grow stronger and stronger, turning the actions into habits. These neural connections make it easier to perform these habits in the future. As these pathways develop, the behavior gets easier, allowing us to perform the behavior without using the thinking centers of our brain. This is why habits are automatic and we don't have to think about them.

Habits form over time, not in an instant. According to psychologist Deann Ware, "When brain cells communicate frequently, the connection between them strengthens and the messages that travel the same pathway in the brain over and over begin to transmit faster. With enough repetition, these behaviors become automatic. Reading, driving, and riding a bike are examples of complicated behaviors that we do automatically because strong neural pathways have formed."[2]

Habits develop when we perform the same behaviors repeatedly. **New habits develop when we establish repetition of new behaviors and create new neural pathways. And the more we repeat new habits, the easier they will become.** Our brains will begin to carve out stronger neural pathways that can help us repeat these habits with more ease. As for the old habits we don't want, over time, the connections we don't use grow weaker and eventually disappear altogether.

Here's a way to think about the process of cultivating new habits. Imagine you have a favorite trail at your local state park. One day, you decide to hike off the path. Instead of walking along a neatly cleared trail, you find yourself walking on tall grass, twigs, and the unforged earth. Walking this new path is going to be more difficult because you are creating a new path. However, suppose each week you decide to walk this same new path. Week after week the hike becomes easier as a new path is established. Step by step you create a new trail.

When you develop new emotional habits, you establish new trails—difficult at first, but easier with time. When you navigate new ways of thinking and behaving, initially it will be challenging. However, the more you repeat these habits, new neural pathways will develop and the habits that were once difficult will become automatic. In this way, we can change our brain; it can evolve and change with our choices.

Even better, sometimes our brain wants to change. When we engage in enjoyable behaviors, our brain releases a chemical called dopamine. Dopamine is called the "feel-good neurotransmitter" because it makes us feel really good! When you practice a new habit that causes positive results, your brain releases dopamine. When you have better relationships and better outcomes as a result of practicing empowering habits, your brain releases more. In other words, our brain has a natural reward system in place (the release of dopamine) that encourages us to take steps towards positive change.

I created a coaching technique I use with clients who have had the feel-good-dopamine experience after practicing empowering habits and want to create even better habits. The coaching technique is called "The Sticky Note Challenge." Here's how it works.

*A Coaching Moment:*
*The Sticky Note Challenge*

For this exercise, I used the habit of **sharing your perspective** as an example. When you try this technique, use this example as an outline and fill in your own responses.

1. Name the emotional habit you want to strengthen.

Example: I want to be brave enough to share my ideas in meetings at work.

2. Describe at least three ways you can shift your thoughts or behaviors and strengthen this habit.

Example: I will share my perspective on both large and small decisions. I will speak up in meetings even if it means creating tension. I will initiate conversations in meetings regarding issues that are important to me.

Now write down the name of the habit on at least seven sticky notes. For example, you can write down "Speak up in meetings." You can also use an acronym like "SUIM." Next, place the sticky notes in places you will see regularly: the mirror in your bathroom, a cosmetic drawer, the dashboard of your car, and so on. For the next several weeks, the sticky notes will remind you to create opportunities when you can practice the new habit. Soon, the new habit will become an old habit, and you can begin again.

## OWN YOUR POWER AND YOUR VOICE

Only you can claim your power and your voice. **Power is not about being able to influence others, but rather is about being able to influence your own life.** Strong emotional habits will help you own your voice and wield power over your circumstances.

I have taught thousands of women how to be empowered and own their voices. Much of what I teach is based on decades of observation and documentation as a psychotherapist. A lot of what I have learned also comes from my personal story. I know what powerlessness feels like, to be afraid to speak up and protect myself. I also know how good it feels to be empowered.

Your voice is the most valuable resource you own. **When a woman has a strong voice, she can amplify her values, act on her opinions, and transform her beliefs into action.** Every woman I have ever met, worked with, or known who has a strong voice also has strong emotional habits. That's why building and sustaining strong emotional habits is incredibly important.

You have power. The question is, are you ready to wield it? You can change your life—I promise. Change one habit at a time, and it will happen. Remind yourself you are not powerless. You have choices. Being empowered is an inside job. It is not something that will come to you from the outside world. It comes from within you.

## CHAPTER 1 IN A NUTSHELL

1. The habit of owning your voice is a pattern of confidently expressing your values, perspective, and who you are at the core.

2. Our emotional habits and voices work in tandem with each other. Emotional habits can either strengthen the innate power of your voice or diminish it. That's why building strong emotional habits is incredibly important and the key to being able to confidently express your voice.

3. An emotional habit is a pattern of thinking or behaving that is on autopilot. We have emotional habits we repeat over and over again, often without realizing how much they influence how we make decisions, how we view ourselves, how they shape the anatomy of our lives and the degree of power we have. For better or worse, our emotional habits have a lot to do with how we show up in the world.

4. Cultivating strong emotional habits is a three-step process. The first step is to be aware of your emotional habits. Awareness is power. Your key to increasing this awareness is naming, describing, and understanding the impact specific emotional habits are having in your life. Awareness empowers you to change negative emotional habits.

5. The second step towards cultivating strong emotional habits is to take control and move old habits out of autopilot. Instead of zoning out and repeating the same habits over and over, we can change how we think, behave, and react. During this stage, we begin to get out of our comfort zone and try new ways of operating.

6. The third step towards building new habits is to practice, practice, practice! Our emotional habits are a lot like

muscles…what we practice grows stronger. This step involves building new emotional muscles into our daily life until they become automatic and little habits become big habits. When we practice new behaviors, we are also creating new neural pathways in our brains that help us repeat new habits with more ease.

7. Only you can claim your power and your voice. Power is not about wielding influence over others, but rather about wielding influence over your life.

8. Becoming empowered is an inside job—you have full control over it.

## QUESTIONS FOR GROUP OR SELF-REFLECTION

1. Name an emotional habit you would like to change or develop.
2. What is one step you can take this week to strengthen this habit?
3. Is there any area of your life where you are in the habit of giving away your power?
4. This week, how can you wield more influence over your life?
5. Do you feel empowered? If so, why?
6. What is one step you can take this week to own your voice?

# CHAPTER 2

# THE HABIT OF TAKING MORE RISKS

## HOW TO GET OUT OF YOUR COMFORT ZONE AND OVERCOME FEAR

What would you do if you weren't ruled by your fear?

I can tell you what I did: I gave a TEDx talk. On a gorgeous fall day in the city of Chicago, I bravely stepped onto the stage, stared into the cameras, and invited the spotlights to illuminate the power of my presence. I felt oddly calm. As I performed my perfectly timed sixteen-minute TEDx talk, I held the gaze of the audience and commanded the room. I nailed my words and the flamenco dance (yes, an actual dance) that was the centerpiece of my message.

As I stepped off the stage and the surge of adrenaline faded, I asked myself, "How did I just do that?" Tears ran down my face as I realized this small-town girl from nowheresville, New Mexico had just accomplished one of her wildest goals. It was a magical moment. I felt like I had just been sprinkled with pixie dust.

Those exhilarating sixteen minutes were preceded by

eighty-seven thousand very difficult, anxiety-producing, pull-my-hair-out minutes. Looking back, the eighty-seven thousand minutes that preceded my TEDx talk were the most important part of the experience. During those laborious minutes, I developed new habits and learned some powerful lessons, such as the importance of getting out of my comfort zone, how to overcome my fear of failure and how to embody my gifts.

I refer to those eighty-seven thousand minutes as one of my best self-improvement boot camps. During that boot camp, one of the biggest personal obstacles I had to overcome was the severe self-doubt that led, at times, to pure panic. Part of preparing for a TEDx talk includes participating in weekly coaching sessions held by the TED organization, a necessary part of preparing for the talk. I worked with three coaches: Nancy, from the TED organization; Tabby Biddle, a women's leadership coach and United Nations Press Fellow; and Brian Burkhart, a nationally known teacher of the power of storytelling and mentor to Shark Tank contestants and TED Speakers.

It's not typical protocol for a speaker to hire three coaches in order to be TEDx-ready. I did so because I was terrified that I would fail and make a fool of myself in front of the audience and cameras. I secretly hoped working with three coaches would somehow protect me from failure. Because I am a perfectionist, I tend to put a lot of pressure on myself. This tendency played a significant role in why failure was so terrifying to me.

I equally dreaded and anticipated each hour of coaching. I longed for feedback that would affirm that I knew what I was doing and was not heading for the edge of a cliff of disaster. Each coach had their own style of feedback. Their comments ranged from sweet and encouraging to downright brutal. In the end, it didn't matter how they packaged their comments. I inevitably ended every coaching session feeling insecure and anxious. My stomach would be in knots, and I would feel a sense of impending doom.

At one point in this agonizing process, I had an embarrassing conversation with my husband Frank, caused by deep fear and anxiety following a particularly challenging coaching session:

**Me**: Honey, I keep hoping that you might have a heart attack or something.

**Frank**: What???

**Me**: Well, if you have a heart attack or something then I will have a legitimate excuse to get out of having to do this dang TEDx talk. I could tell people you are in the hospital and that I needed to be with you.

**Frank**: Well, why can't you have the heart attack or something?

**Me**: That actually never occurred to me, but that could work, too.

Have you ever been so gripped with fear all you wanted was an escape from having to face your fear? After the coaching sessions, I believed I would fail, and I totally underestimated my abilities. Fear does that: it paralyzes us and causes us to believe things about ourselves that are not true. Looking back, I had no good reason to believe I wouldn't give a great talk. I was a skilled and seasoned speaker: I had already spoken to crowds in the thousands, given workshops, and led conferences.

I was an expert in the field of psychology and understood the message I wanted to deliver at TEDx. However, for some reason that I could not figure out at the time, this challenge felt different to me. Giving a TEDx talk took me out of my comfort zone, and my fear was out of control. I was second-guessing myself, and I worried I would not measure up to the standards of a TED speaker. Insecurities I thought I'd tamed ran wild. My fear was overriding my logic.

Fear is a common experience when people take on big challenges. When you say yes to getting out of your comfort zone, you are also saying yes to all of the uncomfortable moments that can come with that decision. But the discomfort you feel can have a greater purpose if you are open to it. The discomfort can teach you how to trust your perspective, manage your fear, and develop your inner resources. These lessons can help you realize you are stronger than you think. Fear feels uncomfortable, but fear can help you grow and expand.

I've been in the room with fear and self-doubt. I don't like it one bit. It makes my stomach churn and my teeth clench. But I choose to leave my comfort zone because I've learned it accelerates my personal growth. In fact, I make it a habit to say yes to at least one thing every year that makes me afraid in order to continually grow and expand. Giving a TEDx talk was one of those challenges. Ultimately, the eighty-seven thousand minutes that led up to giving the TEDx talk were far more valuable than my sixteen minutes of exhilaration in the spotlight. What I learned during those eighty-seven thousand minutes empowered me for a lifetime.

Get into the habit of taking meaningful risks that get you out of your comfort zone. Experience your own sixteen minutes of exhilaration that comes from accomplishing your goal. More importantly, create your own eighty-seven-thousand-minute boot camp where you can cultivate habits that you will use for the rest of your life.

In this chapter, I will provide a roadmap that will guide you towards developing the habit of taking meaningful risks and pursuing bigger challenges, a common habit of empowered women. First, you will learn the connection between perfectionist thinking and the fear of failure. Perfectionist thinking can halt us in our tracks and prevent progress towards goals. We women are more prone to perfectionism than men, so learning how to get past this specific obstacle can eliminate huge roadblocks that can get in our way.

Next, I will help you discover how to tap into your inner resources to manage your fear. Managing different types of fear is half the battle when it comes to taking on bigger challenges. Then you will learn how to own your abilities and stop underestimating yourself. Finally, I will show you how to create a vision statement and mission mantra associated with your big goal. These two tools will provide endless motivation along the way. All these insights and tools will help you become a woman who is willing to fail in order to succeed.

## EMBRACE THE POSSIBILITY OF FAILURE

I have learned in my practice that the fear of failure is one of the biggest reasons why women hold back from taking meaningful risks. These risks that women avoid could launch them into positions of influence or move them closer to their dreams.

When my clients ask me how to pursue their goals without failing, I tell them, "The truth is, you might fail. Saying yes to risk means saying yes to the possibility of failure. Empowered women accept that failing is part of the success equation."

I have learned a lot from my male peers about how to be more bold, uninhibited, and willing to embrace the possibility of failure. Here's an example. For weeks, I'd been wrestling with whether to invest a substantial amount of money in my business and create a more contemporary online presence. I asked my husband Frank how he takes risks with such ease. I've noticed he doesn't seem to "get stuck in his head" as much as I do when it comes to calculating whether to say yes to a high-risk opportunity. One evening during dinner I asked Frank for his opinion regarding my business investment. After gathering information about the details of the decision, he quickly developed a perspective on the issue and confidently recommended I move forward with the financial investment. A problem that I'd been wrestling with for weeks took my husband less than fifteen minutes to solve. When I asked him how he came to his decision so swiftly, he shared a metaphor with me.

> Imagine growing up playing a game where 25% success is good, 30% is exceptional, and at 40% you are a superstar. A game where perfection is not the aim, but simply being in the game and trying to get to 30% or more is the goal. This is the game of baseball, which I grew up playing. Everybody who plays baseball knows they are not going to "bat a thousand": that is, they are not pursuing perfection. Yet, they step up to the plate, ready to bat, unafraid, trying to get a hit.

His baseball metaphor taught me I needed to stop pursuing a perfect outcome and instead pursue the possibility of just hitting the ball. His answer helped me realize how my bad habit of perfectionist thinking had been blocking my ability to move into action. **Perfectionist thinking is a tendency to set personal standards that are so high either they cannot be met, or only with great difficulty**. It's a tendency to see even minor imperfections in oneself as not acceptable or horrible. Perfectionist thinking can keep us from stepping up to the plate because of a self-imposed pressure to always hit the ball, which is impossible, as any professional baseball player can tell you. Perfectionist thinking prevents us from taking risks that can lead to realizing our success and ambitions.

I needed to let go of perfectionist thinking and embrace the possibility of failure in order to win. Frank's clever response provided a working model on how to approach challenges that include a level of risk.

A "good enough" mentality almost always outperforms an "I need to do it perfectly" mentality. I call this way of thinking the **Good Enough Equation. Don't put pressure on yourself to never make mistakes. Instead, give yourself permission to be "good enough." To do so, set aside any belief that says you need to achieve your goals perfectly.** Don't wait until you have all the answers. Instead, step up to the bat and give it your best swing.

*Achieving the Good Enough Equation*

1. First, when you take a risk, accept you might not hit the ball. Perfectionism is not the goal. Stepping up to the plate and taking your best swing is the goal.
2. Second, your goal is not to bat one thousand (in regular speak, hitting the ball 100% of the time). If you don't hit the ball, it's not a reflection of your worth. Failure is part of the game. Failure is normal and reflects that you have the guts to take a chance.
3. Third, sometimes when you play, you won't score. When this happens, dust yourself off and prepare to step up to the plate again.
4. Perfectionism will lead to immobility. Get out of the dugout and play the game.
5. If you want to score, you must be willing to step up to the plate. Don't overthink it or wait until you are perfectly ready. Get out of your head and just do it.

**Successful women are willing to fail in order to succeed. They set aside perfectionism and give it their best shot.** Don't hold back from taking the chances that could launch you into a position of influence or move you closer to your dreams. Instead, move into action and set aside any expectation of perfection. You're more likely to succeed if you're willing to fail.

## OVERCOME FEAR BY TAPPING INTO YOUR INNER RESOURCES

Empowered women consistently take bold risks. However, the bigger the risk you take, the greater the fear you must face. Saying yes to bold opportunities means saying yes to the fear that comes with them. But fear does not have to overpower you. The key to controlling fear is understanding the type of fear you are dealing with and then tapping into your inner resources to manage it.

Fear is typically triggered by a threat to our well-being; it can be real or imagined. Whether real or imagined, fear is very upsetting and uncomfortable. It is typically an ongoing undercurrent of discomfort. In my practice, I have observed specific fears that emerge when women take on the kinds of challenges that get them out of their comfort zones.

- The fear of failure
- The fear of disappointing others
- The fear of not being good enough
- The fear of not being perfect
- The fear of rejection

- The fear of being seen

Other fears emerge when women choose to take risks, but these are the most common. Furthermore, a specific person will tend to experience certain types of fears more than others. For instance, I am more likely to struggle with the fear of not being good enough rather than the fear of failure. Because I know this about myself, I expect to struggle with this particular fear when I take on a big challenge. Identifying the types of fears you are more likely to experience will make it easier to manage them.

*Identify Your Fears*

Start by using the following coaching questions to shed light on your fears. Identifying your fears can help you manage them.

1. Think about a time, past or present, when you took on a challenge that pushed you out of your comfort zone. Perhaps you said yes to a new opportunity, pitched an idea to your boss, or left your job to start your own business.

2. Next, identify any fears you experienced when you took on that challenge. For example, the fear of rejection, failure, and so on. Use the list of fears to help you if needed.

3. Looking back at that moment in your life, if you

could respond to the fears and offer yourself some advice, what would it be?

Identifying what kinds of fears you are feeling when you take on a big challenge can help you control them. There is something powerful about giving a fear a name and then talking to yourself about it. Naming your fear lessens the fear's power over you and puts the fear into perspective.

*Identify Your Inner Resources*

Regardless of whether your fear became a reality, I'll bet your inner resources kicked in and helped you manage the experience. An inner resource is a preexisting strength that surfaces during demanding, stressful, or challenging moments. Inner resources come in all shapes and sizes. Here is a list of just a few examples of inner resources.

### List of Inner Resources

Tenacity | Intelligence | Endurance
Courage | Creativity | Independence
Passion | Discipline | Strong Work Ethic
Resilience | Resourcefulness | Persistence | Flexibility
Positive Mindset | Inner Strength | Determination

I come from a small town in New Mexico where just finishing high school was a big accomplishment. Many of my classmates dropped out of school because of drugs, teen pregnancy, and mental health issues. Because of my past, I never imagined I would achieve a higher education. When I arrived at college, I had a bad case of imposter syndrome. **Imposter syndrome is the feeling that you are in a place where you don't belong because you aren't good enough— even though you are.**

Have you ever felt like that before?

I was frequently overwhelmed by the academic demands of college. I decided I would focus on one challenge at a time to keep from getting overwhelmed. When I got stuck, I asked for help. I kept a dictionary in my backpack to look up all the words I did not understand—and there were many. If I got a grade I did not like, I made an appointment with my professor to discuss how I could improve on the next assignment.

Growing up on a farm taught me the power of working twelve-hour days, and I used that work ethic to help me succeed. When my peers went out on the weekends, I went to the library to work. When they were relaxing with a movie midweek, I opted to review my notes or study. I was tenacious and determined, knowing these attributes were in my control. Our inner resources surface during demanding and stressful moments. In the story I'm telling you now, I was using my inner resources to manage the fear, the self-doubt, and the feeling of not being good enough for college.

You also have a wealth of inner resources that you can tap into next time you pursue something that matters to you. Take a moment to think about the many challenges you've already conquered. Have you raised kids, organized events, or completed your education? Have you worked through a personal tragedy, survived a tough upbringing, or successfully competed for a job? Your inner resources surfaced during those demanding times.

Every challenge you've faced required you to tap into your inner resources. The next time fear surfaces, tap into these preexisting strengths. Remind yourself you've been through difficult times before. **When you're thinking of taking on a challenge, don't wait until the fear subsides before you move into action. Instead, assume fear is part of the process.** When the time comes to work through fear, you will be surprised how your inner resources kick in and help you navigate the experience. Trust yourself. You are stronger than you think.

*Own Your Gifts and Abilities*

In my practice, I have noticed that when my female clients are considering taking on a challenge, such as starting their own business, moving into positions of leadership, or spearheading a cause they are passionate about, they tend to overestimate what's necessary to accomplish their goals and underestimate their ability to achieve them. I see this pattern frequently, where women are less likely than men to own their gifts and abilities.

There is fascinating research that reveals why this pattern is more common among women than men. In 2008, Hewlett-Packard published an internal report about the different perspectives of men and women when they were applying for a job.[1] In their report, they found if a company posts a position with ten job qualifications, men are likely to apply if they have six out of the ten job qualifications. In contrast, women who were considering applying to the same job only applied if they had all ten of the job qualifications. In other words, men applied if they had 60 percent of the qualifications; women only applied if they met 100 percent of the qualifications. **Thus, women would often apply only when they felt one hundred percent confident that they were a good fit by having all ten job qualifications.** This Hewlett-Packard study revealed that women were more likely to overestimate the job tasks and underestimate their ability to accomplish the tasks. Their research suggests this pattern in women occurs not just in the workplace, but in general when women are considering pursuing greater accomplishments.

In short, the Hewlett-Packard study indicated men were more likely to overestimate their abilities and performance while women were more likely to underestimate their abilities and performance. Because of this difference, it's likely that underqualified and underprepared men are more likely to take risks and overqualified and overly prepared women are more likely to hold back from taking risks.

The good news is this: I have found that when women become aware of this tendency, they can do something about it. They can stop underestimating themselves and start acknowledging their gifts and capabilities. They recognize how perfectionist thinking can get in the way of their pursuits and become more willing to embrace the Good Enough Equation. They are less likely to play it safe and instead take more chances.

*A Coaching Moment:*
*Own Your Gifts and Abilities*

Have you fully embraced your gifts and abilities, or does perfectionist thinking still keep you from moving into action? The following coaching tool will help you shed light on whether you are fully owning your abilities.

1. Identify a dream or goal you've thought of pursuing that would require taking on some risk. Try to pick a challenge that would put you out of your comfort zone. Think big. What dream have you always wanted to pursue but have been postponing?
Here are some ideas to help you brainstorm.

- Pitching a business idea that you have
- Moving to a new state
- Starting a charity that you are passionate about
- Writing a book
- Going to graduate school
- Changing careers
- Starting your own company
- Launching your own blog, radio show, or podcast

2. Now, imagine that at this moment you are deciding whether or not to pursue your dream. Saying yes to your dream also means accepting a certain level of risk, and getting out of your comfort zone. As you imagine making the decision, what's your internal dialogue?

MARGO TIRADO

3. Do you believe you can accomplish your goal? Why or why not?

4. Do you feel qualified to take on this risk? Do you trust your ability to accomplish your goal or dream? Why or why not?

Earlier in this chapter, I talked about how women are more likely than men to underestimate their abilities and overestimate the task. Take a moment to reflect on your answers. Did you underestimate your ability to pursue your dream—or did you own your capabilities?

Hopefully, you acknowledged your capabilities and now feel convinced that you are perfectly capable of pursuing opportunities that matter to you. If not, don't wait to move into action until you feel completely confident. Instead, get started on the task and trust that your inner resources will help you work through each step toward your goal.

## ROBIN, THE LITTLE ENGINE THAT COULD

I worked with a coaching client named Robin (not her real name) who dreamed about opening an antique store, but she didn't believe she had the skills necessary to own her own business. Robin's self-doubt immobilized her. I knew Robin well and was certain the only thing keeping Robin from her dream was believing in herself.

She had never climbed this particular mountain, but she already had everything she needed inside of herself to do so. It reminded me of the children's story *The Little Engine That*

*Could.*[2] In the story, the Little Engine pulls a train filled with toys and treats over a high mountain through the power of hope and self-determination. Initially, the little train is not sure she can accomplish the task but is willing to try. During the climb the little engine repeats a mantra to herself: "I think I can, I think I can." This simple mantra helps the little train pull forward, one step (or track) at a time until she ultimately succeeds. For Robin, the "mountain" of starting her own business would require her to believe in herself and take one step at a time while holding onto hope that she would succeed.

My job was to help Robin climb her mountain one step at a time until she realized she already had the inner resources within her to accomplish her goal. I decided to help Robin break down monumental steps into smaller, more manageable steps. To do so, we created a weekly schedule of tasks she would accomplish related to opening her own antique business. The first task was exploring all the possible locations she could open her business. She spent a weekend creating a list of places she could rent and was pleasantly surprised to find several affordable spaces within five miles of her home. Next, I had Robin work on creating a budget for her business. Soon after, she asked her niece to teach her how to use QuickBooks so she could keep track of the budget. Each week, we picked out another small task for Robin to accomplish—one more small step up the big mountain.

Robin reached out to several friends and found someone to set up a business web page and help with social media marketing. Robin's engine began to gain steam as she steadily moved her way down the tracks toward owning her own business. She soon realized she had a knack for networking and problem-solving. I helped her write a vision statement and a mission mantra to coincide with her goal. (I'll share more about these items later in this chapter.) Week by week, taking on small tasks one at a time, she worked through her fear and self-doubt and began to own her capabilities. When Robin finally opened her antique business, she realized she had always been capable, she just needed to stop underestimating herself and learn how to break down a mountainous task into smaller, more manageable tasks that seem less frightening.

It's normal to struggle with fear and self-doubt when it comes to taking big risks. I have coached trailblazers who inspired significant changes in their field of expertise. **What set them apart was a willingness to fail in order to succeed, the determination to take one step at a time, and assuming self-doubt and fear were part of the process.** Every one of these brave women struggled with fear and self-doubt as they took steps towards their goal. Despite their fear, they took one step at a time, broke down each task into manageable goals, and worked with fear as it occurred. These were everyday women, just like you. If you have a dream you want to accomplish, take one step at a time. It's okay to start with the belief, "I think I can." Soon, you will be on top of your mountain saying, "Wow! I can!"

Remember, you are fully capable of achieving your goals. If a mountain seems too big, take one step at a time until you climb it.

## CREATE INSPIRATION WITH A VISION STATEMENT AND A MISSION MANTRA

So far in this chapter, you have learned that you must be willing to fail in order to succeed—which requires you to set aside perfectionism; you must activate your inner resources in order to overcome fear; and it helps to break down monumental tasks into small more manageable tasks.

The final step in the process of learning to take risks is to learn how to create a vision statement and a mission mantra. **A vision statement is a descriptive statement that reflects why you want to pursue a specific goal. A mission mantra is a simple statement you can say to yourself when you feel stuck or unmotivated to pursue your goal.** These tools will help you remain steadfast and mindful of the reason you said yes to a big challenge.

When I decided that I wanted to embark on the journey to give a TEDx talk, I needed to get clear on why I wanted to do it. I also needed a method of maintaining momentum when emotional fatigue, rejection, and self-doubt set in.

First, I created a vision statement—a simple but descriptive statement that reflects the reason I wanted to give a TEDx talk. This was my vision statement:

**Vision Statement**: I have a voice that has been silent for too long. It's time to be heard. I want to use my voice to empower and encourage a million women in my lifetime. Giving a TEDx talk will help accomplish this goal. It is time to unleash the power of the feminine voice—my own and others.

Next, I created a mission mantra—a simple statement I could say to myself when I felt discouraged or unmotivated along the way. My TEDx mentor Tabby Biddle recommended this mantra:

**Mission Mantra**: Just stay in the process.

At first, I thought it was a bit too simple, but soon I realized it was both potent and powerful, and the simplicity of the mantra made it easier to recall. It reminded me of the Little Engine's mantra, "I think I can, I think I can." As I prepared for my TEDx talk, I would repeat "just stay in the process" as I battled each moment of self-doubt.

I put my vision statement and mission mantra on two huge sticky notes and stuck them on my desk where they were always visible. Reading them kept me energized and focused, and they encouraged me throughout the long and challenging process.

The first step in the process was applying to TEDx organizations to compete to give a talk. (TEDx events are planned locally and independently under the TED umbrella, and you must apply to give your talk at one.) I was rejected from seven TEDx organizations before I was finally accepted to TEDx Grant Park in Chicago. During this application—and rejection—process, my vision statement, and mission mantra kept me from quitting and helped me stay the course, despite my self-doubt.

Vision statements and mission mantras are great for all kinds of personal goals. I created a pair of them when I downsized my counseling practice and moved from full-time to part-time hours. I was burned out and needed to slow down and simplify my life. It seemed counterintuitive to downsize a business I'd spent twenty years building, but I also knew I needed to stop the overly busy cycle I was living in and rethink how I could use my time and desire to impact women more strategically. As my income steadily declined, I reflected on them. Here's the vision statement and mission mantra from that period in my life:

**Vision statement**: I want to simplify my life and feel more present and mindful. I want to use this time to create clarity regarding what I want to do next in my work with women.

**Mission mantra**: Take the next step by faith.

These words helped me stay the course as I restructured my career, even though I was often afraid.

*Create Your Own Vision Statement*
*and Mission Mantra*

These words provide tremendous comfort and perspective when things get tough. Here's how to create your own. First, you will identify your goal, then you will develop a vision statement connected to your goal. Do this by reflecting on the following questions. As you respond to each question, don't overthink it. Rather, respond to the reason your heart wants to do it.

1. What is the goal or challenge you have decided to say yes to?

2. Why do you want to pursue this goal?

3. Why is this particular goal important to you?

4. What would it mean if you accomplished this goal?

5. How can you combine your answers to create your vision statement? It can be complex or simple. Create one that speaks to your heart.

6. Next, create a mission mantra, or a simple statement you can say to yourself when you feel stuck, discouraged, or unmotivated to pursue your goal? Think about a simple phrase you would tell a friend needing encouragement to pursue her goal. An example of a mission mantra would be, "Just stay in the process."

You just created your first vision statement and mission mantra. Way to go! I suggest writing them down on a big bright sticky note and placing them in a location you see daily. Reflect on them when you need motivation, are struggling with self-doubt, or need to remember why what you are doing is a risk worth taking.

When you pursue your goals and say yes to meaningful challenges, you will also strengthen your inner confidence. A self-imposed boot camp can activate a season of personal growth where you can discover that you are stronger than you think. During boot camp, develop habits that will help accomplish your goals: minimize perfectionism, own your abilities and your gifts. Always be willing to accept failure as part of the process. When fear kicks in, tap into your inner resources. These habits will empower you to accomplish your goals and have a bigger voice in the world.

## CHAPTER 2 IN A NUTSHELL

1. The habit of taking risks is a pattern of pursuing meaningful risks and greater opportunities.

2. Empowered women frequently take bold risks. But the bigger the risk you take, the greater the fear. Saying yes to bold opportunities means saying yes to the fear that comes with it.

3. Don't wait for fear to subside before you move into action and pursue your goals. Fear does not have to overpower you. The key to controlling fear is understanding the type of fear you're dealing with and then tapping into your inner resources to manage it.

4. An inner resource is a preexisting strength that surfaces during stressful or challenging moments. Here are just a few

examples of an inner resource: tenacity, intelligence, organization, courage, creativity, passion, and discipline.

5. A "good enough" mentality typically outperforms an "I need to do it perfectly" mentality. This is the Good Enough Equation. Don't wait until you have all the answers. Don't put pressure on yourself to not make mistakes. Instead, give yourself permission to be "good enough." You can do that by setting aside any belief that says you need to achieve your goals perfectly.

6. When you take a risk, you might not "hit the ball." Perfectionism is not the goal; stepping up to the plate and trying to score is. Failure is part of the game and not a reflection of your worth or ability.

7. Empowered women are willing to fail in order to succeed.

8. Research shows that women are more likely than men to overestimate what is necessary to accomplish their goals and underestimate their ability to achieve them. With this in mind, own your abilities and boldly pursue your goals even if you believe you are underqualified. (You aren't.)

9. It's easier to overcome fear when you take something big and scary and break it down into less scary steps. Next time you're working towards a goal, break down each task into small measurable steps. Then work through each task one at a time. It will be easier to climb your mountain when simply focusing on one step at a time.

10. A vision statement is a descriptive statement that reflects why you want to pursue a specific goal. A mission mantra is a short sentence or phrase you can say to yourself when you feel stuck, discouraged, or unmotivated to pursue your goal. Creating a vision statement and mission mantra can help you stay motivated and determined to pursue meaningful risks.

## QUESTIONS FOR GROUP OR SELF-REFLECTION

1. What would you do if you weren't afraid?
2. Are you willing to fail in order to succeed?
3. What is the gift you want to share with the world?
4. Talk about a time when you succeeded at something that was important to you. What did you learn about yourself during that time?
5. Talk about a time when you failed at something that was important to you. What did you learn about yourself during that time?
6. What inner resources can you tap into when fear emerges?
7. Sometimes others can help us see our strengths that we have yet to own. Ask a friend whom you trust the following question: "What do you think are some of my unique gifts or abilities?"
8. What is the most meaningful risk you have taken in your life?

# CHAPTER 3
# THE HABIT OF LOWERING YOUR TOLERANCE FOR CRAP
## HOW TO REVERSE THE HABIT OF CODEPENDENCY

I will never forget the summer I finally reached my threshold for crap and stopped making excuses for other people's intolerable behavior toward me. The year was 2005, and I was back home in Santa Fe, New Mexico for a family visit. When I'm back in my hometown, I try to see as many family members as possible—but with over a hundred family members in the area and a limited amount of time, it isn't possible to see them all.

Upon arrival, I realized I had forgotten to inform one of my family members, named Manuel (not his real name), that I would be in town. Although we had a difficult history stretching back to childhood, I always made a point to visit him when I came back home.

I immediately called him to see if he had time to get together. Shortly into our conversation, he berated me for calling him at the last minute, lashed out with a list of cruel accusations about my character, and labeled me a terrible family member. He finished the one-way conversation with a flurry of nasty obscenities before abruptly hanging up the phone. I felt hurt and confused but mostly I felt terrible guilt. I quickly assumed the blame for his anger and promptly called him back to apologize. When he answered the phone, I tried to share my point of view but only managed to speak a few words before I was quickly cut off, met with another string of stinging expletives, and then a "click" on the other end of the phone. He indicted me without a trial, and I let him.

Can you guess what I did? Yup, I called Manuel back several more times to apologize. I was determined to extinguish his rage and restore harmony between us. But he was determined to put me in my place. He was upset I had called him at the last minute and felt excluded from having time with me. We engaged in a perverse cycle where I repeatedly called him begging to be understood and he berated me and then hung up the phone. Eventually, he stopped picking up the phone at all. When the call went to voicemail, I left yet another contrite apology, acknowledged his disappointment, and beseeched him to call me back so we could reconcile. He never called back, and I walked around with a pit in my stomach for the remainder of my visit in New Mexico, playing his acidic words over and over again in my head, convinced that I had done something horribly wrong.

This was not the first time I endured an explosive interaction with Manuel. He'd physically and emotionally abused me throughout my childhood. I couldn't protect myself from him as a child and had not yet learned how to protect myself as an adult. As an adult, I believed that if I showed enough kindness and pleased him, we could have a relationship. No matter how many times I did this, the outcome had always been the same. I disappointed him and he became angry with me. However, this time, something began to shift within me, and my protective instincts finally began to take root. I thought more about our interaction and realized I was owning what was not mine to own—his inability to control his anger. I started to think about what I was and was not okay with, rather than simply submitting to my desire for harmony. I began to give myself permission to be honest about the true nature of my relationship with Manuel and acknowledge it was toxic. I was finally giving myself permission to protect myself. I was forty years old. It was time to stop tolerating crap, and I was starting with my relationship with Manuel.

Have you ever been in a relationship where you kept making excuses for somebody's intolerable behavior? That's what I had been doing in this relationship for years. I was hoping Manuel would eventually change, but I was the one who needed to change my codependent habits. Simply put, **a codependent person seeks out experiences that give them a feeling of being loved, valued, and needed**. **This pattern usually includes taking crap that should not be tolerated.** The drive to act in these ways stems from childhood when they felt unloved, insecure, or alone. They bring what worked for them in childhood, meeting the needs and expectations of others, with them into adulthood.

I was confusing compassion for having a high tolerance for crap. This was a codependent pattern I needed to change. Instead of making excuses for his anger, I needed to set boundaries by communicating what I was and was not okay with. When we were children, Manuel and I lived in a harsh, unpredictable, and volatile environment. I understood how this environment could mess with one's emotional wellbeing. But we were both adults now. He needed to own his anger and I needed to stop making excuses for his anger. **I needed to take responsibility for my part in our disagreement, but it was not my job to take responsibility for his emotions.**

Our bodies often tell us the truth about our circumstances. My body told me the truth regarding my relationship with Manuel. I started to think about how my body felt when I was near him and realized it was chronically uncomfortable in his presence. Whenever I was near him, I always felt tense, unsettled, and a little afraid. I could sense the anger in him just beneath the surface, always ready to emerge. This relationship had been causing anxiety in me for a long time. My body revealed the truth about what I wanted but had been unwilling to admit for years—I didn't want to be near him.

Acknowledging what I needed kicked me out of the "nice girl syndrome" and into the "healthy woman" track. I made a decision that eventually brought me great peace. I gave myself permission to end my relationship with Manuel. Ending the relationship was a huge step for me—**I was usually aware of how I felt but typically not aware of what I needed.** Knowing what I needed was unfamiliar to me. Acting on it was even harder. Does this sound familiar to you? We codependents have great difficulty acknowledging what we need, and even greater difficulty asking for it.

As I created better boundaries with him, listened to my

body, and stopped owning his emotions and justifying bad behavior, I became more empowered. I stopped feeling helpless when I stopped being helpless. I always buy a new piece of turquoise jewelry when I'm in New Mexico, but that summer I returned with something I needed even more: a collection of habits that empowered me for a lifetime.

**Codependency and being empowered are psychological opposites. Codependent habits breed helplessness and self-devaluation. Empowering habits amplify a woman's power and increase her self-confidence.** Codependency will always short circuit a women's power and undermine her voice. Simply put, you can't be codependent and empowered.

This chapter is devoted to helping you develop the habit of lowering your tolerance for crap, which means creating a pattern of setting healthy boundaries and not tolerating toxic behavior. You will find a self-assessment that will help identify if you have codependent tendencies. I'll shed light on how codependent patterns evolve and more importantly, how to change them. I provide a detailed description of five game-changing habits that will dismantle patterns of codependency: stating what you need, deciding what you will and will not tolerate, dismantling people-pleasing tendencies, holding and releasing emotions, and creating an identity from within. These insights will help you plug into your power, strengthen boundaries, and build a resolve to decrease any toleration of intolerable nonsense.

## EMOTIONAL NEGLECT AND THE BIRTH OF CODEPENDENCE

Why are some people susceptible to codependency in their adult relationships? While it's not the same for everyone, codependency typically starts when a child experiences emotional neglect: that is, when a parent ignores or is unable to respond to the emotional needs of the child. When children experience neglect or feel invisible, ignored, or unsafe, they begin to believe they don't matter. More specifically, they believe that what they think and feel doesn't matter. In response, the wise child develops "a sixth sense" (the ability to perceive what others want from them). The child uses their sixth sense to develop behavior that will give them a feeling of being loved and secure. For example, the child might become overly eager to meet the needs and expectations of others. As such, they may be stringently obedient to, or improperly caregiving toward their parents. They might learn that over-performing or being "the perfect child" will provide at least a brief feeling of being noticed. The wise child performs the behavior that will give them a feeling of being loved, valued, and needed to lessen the experience of neglect.

Fast forward: when the child becomes an adult, they unknowingly replicate the same set of behaviors in their adult relationships. For example, they might become overly submissive, excessively caregiving, or otherwise overperforming in relationships. Rocking the boat is harder for them because they've been groomed to avoid tension. Neglect is familiar to them, so they tend to make excuses for the people who hurt them. They feel most secure when their "approval rating" is high, and they worry (like I did with Manuel) when others get upset with them.

Codependent adults struggle with being who they really are because they believe that person is unlovable. They seek to please others by anticipating their needs. They say "yes" when they want to say "no." They struggle with knowing what they need and have an even harder time asking for it. These are just a few of the behaviors a codependent might bring with them into adulthood.

Does any of this sound familiar? If so, you might be struggling with codependency. You are not alone. Many of us do.

The problem lies in the instability of the habits codependents use, because they provide only a temporary and tenuous feeling of security. They deliver a sense of adequacy that is too dependent on the responses of others. However, when we build a solid understanding of who we are to ourselves rather than to others, and when we build an identity from within, we start to change these habits.

As a recovering codependent, I can relate to the insecurity that stems from creating an identity based on temporary encounters. I can also attest to the emotional freedom that comes from breaking free of codependent habits and the power that's birthed from creating an identity from within. I can't wait to share how to create these changes. But first, let's put a magnifying glass on these patterns in order to see more clearly what needs to change.

〜

## DO YOU HAVE A HIGH TOLERANCE FOR CRAP? A SELF-ASSESSMENT

Codependent thinking lurks just beneath the surface of our interactions with others and is often thinly veiled in kindness, patience, and other niceties. When these niceties are motivated by a need to feel secure, they can be harmful. Melody Beattie, leading authority on codependency and author of *Codependent No More*,[1] describes these subtle behaviors and what they look like under a magnifying glass.

Here is an abbreviated list from Melody Beattie's literature that describes codependent habits, along with a process I created to use the list to identify codependent habits you'd like to change in yourself.

*A Coaching Moment:*
*Codependency Self-Assessment*

**1. Identify Your Behaviors.** Read this list from beginning to end. As you read, take notice of any patterns that are familiar. You might feel a little overwhelmed. If so, remember to be kind and compassionate with yourself.

- Do I think and feel responsible for other people and for other people's feelings, actions, choices, wants, needs, well-being, or lack of well-being?
- Do I feel compelled to help other people solve their problems, such as offering unwanted advice, giving

a rapid-fire series of suggestions, or fixing their feelings?

- Do I anticipate other people's needs and wonder why others don't do the same for me?
- Do I find myself saying yes when I want to say no, and do things I don't really want to be doing?
- Do I provide more than my fair share of the work or do things other people are capable of doing for themselves?
- Do I have difficulty knowing what I want and need, and when I do, telling myself what I want and need is not important?
- Do I chronically try to please others instead of myself?
- Do I find it easier to express anger about injustices done to others but have difficulty expressing anger when injustices happen to me?
- Do I feel safest when giving?
- Do I feel uncomfortable or guilty when somebody takes care of me?
- Do I feel sad because I give so much to others, but nobody gives to me?
- Do I find myself attracted to or frequently in relationships with needy people?
- Do I abandon my routine to respond to or do something for somebody else?
- Do I overcommit myself because I have difficulty saying no?
- Do I feel I am not quite good enough?

- Do I feel guilty about spending money on myself or doing lavish things for myself?
- Do I take things personally?
- Do I have a lot of "shoulds" and feel a lot of guilt?
- Do I derive a sense of self-worth from helping others?
- Do I believe other people can't or don't love me?
- Do I desperately seek love and approval?
- Do I seek love from people who are incapable of loving?
- Do I believe other people are never there for me?
- Do I stay in relationships that don't work?
- Do I keep letting people hurt me?
- Do I tolerate behavior I shouldn't tolerate?

**2. Take a Break**. When you're finished reading the list, walk away from it for twenty-four hours. Doing so will give you time to digest any new insights. Plan on returning to this self-assessment the following day.

**3. Identify Patterns**. Return to the list and read it again, but this time place an asterisk on any pattern you identify as your own.

**4. Focus**. Narrow down the list with asterisks to three that you want to break free from. Focus on changing these three behaviors first. Don't worry about the rest of the list for now.

**5. Action**. Ask yourself: "What are three things I am ready to do this week to start changing these habits?" Then commit to changing these patterns one day at a time.

**Self-awareness is power.** If you're even a little bit more aware of any tendency to build an identity based on your interactions with others, you're now more empowered.

**There's power in knowing what you want to change in your life.** Now that you have awareness, you need skills that will help reverse codependency and build a solid understanding of who you are in relationship to yourself rather than to others. One of my clients named these skills the Magic Five because they effectively helped her dismantle codependency habits.

## THE FIVE MAGIC HABITS TO DISMANTLE CODEPENDENCY

There are five game-changing habits that will dismantle patterns of codependency: stating what you need, deciding what you will and will not tolerate, saying no to people-pleasing habits, learning how to hold and release emotions, and creating an identity from the inside out. These habits will help create relational boundaries, empower you to develop an identity from within, and help break the habit of codependency.

～

*Magic Habit 1.*
*State What You Need*

The first of the five magic habits sets the foundation for the next four. You need to know what you need and be willing to ask for it. It sounds so simple, but if you've got a little codependent living inside you, chances are you're squirming in your seat right now at the thought of magnifying your needs. Codependents are notorious for ignoring and outright dismissing their needs.

Before my own wake-up call, I often knew how I was feeling but rarely knew what I needed. **Knowing how you feel is very different from stating what you need.** It's important to put your needs into the relationship equation.

If you were raised in an environment where your emotional needs were ignored, dismissed, or minimized, then having your emotional needs ignored, dismissed, and minimized probably feels normal to you. Except those feelings shouldn't be normal. Your needs matter. Your feelings matter. You matter!

The first habit of breaking free from codependent thinking is to become conscious of what you need and then respond to it. It's time to focus some of your compassion inward. To do this, create a new lens that sees you have needs and they matter, your needs are not less important than the needs of others, and it's okay to include your wishes into the decision-making process.

*A Coaching Moment:*
*How to Develop the Habit*
*of Stating What You Need*

Stating what you need will empower you to shape your experiences. More importantly, every time you ask for what you need you will embody the belief that you matter. The habit of stating what you need can be organized into three simple steps:

1. Ask yourself "What do I need?" Don't minimize it or talk yourself out of it. Simply describe what you need.

2. Give yourself permission to accept that what you need is valid. This is hard! If you're having difficulty, remind yourself of the core beliefs: you have needs and they matter, your needs are not less important than the needs of others, and it's okay to include your perspective in the decision-making process.

3. Respond to what you need. It might be something you need to ask for. It might be something you can do for yourself. The goal is simple…respond to your need.

Knowing and asking for what you need will be a game-changing habit. I promise. When you've developed this emotional muscle, you will be ready for the second of the Five Magic Habits—being clear about what you will and will not tolerate.

*Magic Habit 2.*
*Decide What You Will and Will Not Tolerate*

Tapping into what you need will help build the next habit —establishing boundaries. **A boundary is a line that marks what is and is not okay with you**. One way to do this is to ask yourself, "What am I tolerating, saying yes to, or submitting to that I shouldn't?"

**Personal boundaries are the limits we create that determine how others behave towards us and how we respond to others when they pass those limits.** Water will always flow to the lowest point: the lower the slope, the lower the water will travel. Boundaries work the same way; others will often "flow to the lowest point" we have set for what we will and will not tolerate. Not everybody will, but some will. They might do it unconsciously, but they will do it, nonetheless. It's our job to communicate our boundaries to others. Only we own that power. We are always teaching others how to interact with us, and this includes communicating what we are and are not okay with.

One of my coaching clients, Kita (not her real name), was always giving in to her overbearing mother-in-law. One day in session she was expressing her frustration regarding her mother-in-law, who insisted Kita call her every day to check in. She called her mother-in-law daily and without fail, even though she resented it. Their thirty-minute phone calls were typically a one-way conversation where Kita listened to her mother-in-law criticize others and spew a negative view of the world. This routine frustrated Kita, who was a busy mother of three young children and a part-time teacher with a limited amount of free time.

I asked Kita, "Why don't you just stop calling her every day?"

She responded with a string of reasons she believed left her with no choice:

- "Oh, but I would feel guilty if I didn't call her."
- "What if she gets upset with me?"
- "It's only twenty to thirty minutes a day."
- "She's lonely and she really counts on hearing from me."
- "I don't want to hurt her feelings."

It never even occurred to my lovely client that she did indeed have a choice in the matter and control over her decision. She hadn't yet realized she had given all her decision-making power to her mother-in-law and kept none for herself. Her mother-in-law was simply "flowing to Kita's lowest point."

Kita and I began to explore the reasons she was having such difficulty saying no to her mother-in-law. After a bit of coaching, Kita began to identify the beliefs that were keeping her from setting boundaries:

- She knew what she needed but felt uncomfortable asking for it.
- She was avoiding the discomfort of her mother-in-law's disapproval.

- She believed her mother-in-law's needs mattered more than her own.
- She did not want to be unkind to her mother-in-law or hurt her feelings.

Kita was having difficulty defining what she was and was not okay with. It was time for Kita to check in with herself and ask, "What do I need"? We spent some time discussing the anatomy of codependency, the habits that sustain it, and how her beliefs were rooted in these habits. Eventually, I asked her, "Kita what do you need and what are you tolerating that you shouldn't be?" I was inspired by her responses in our conversation:

**Kita**: "I need to call her less often, maybe once or twice a week. I also need her to ask me how I'm doing. It would help if the conversation moved in both directions. Of course, she can reach out to me if she truly needs something."

**Me**: "How do you feel about setting these limits?"

**Kita**: "Guilty, but relieved."

**Me**: "Are you willing to put into practice what you need and what you are not okay with?"

**Kita**: "It's not going to be easy, but I am going to do it."

Revising her commitment to her mother-in-law gave Kita

the freedom that comes from setting healthy limits, adding her needs to the relationship equation, and feeling less driven by the need for approval. It was the beginning of the end of her codependent thinking.

The habit of setting boundaries sounds like an easy task but it's often more complex. Sometimes boundaries need to have flexible gates where others can come and go. Sometimes they need to be more like a twelve-foot cement wall with no entrance. The act of setting boundaries requires discernment and the ability to balance the needs of others with your own.[2]

*Magic Habit 3.*
*Say No to People-Pleasing Habits*

**People-pleasing is the habit of perpetually responding to the wishes, expectations, or demands of others while neglecting your own.** Of course, we all want to do things that make our loved ones happy. That's part of being in a healthy relationship. However, chronic people-pleasing rooted in the need to feel affirmed, loved, or secure is not healthy because it's rooted in the belief that your worth comes from meeting the needs of others.

If you experienced emotional neglect as a child, one of the ways you might have adapted to your environment was by figuring out what others wanted from you and then responding to their wishes or demands. **Your emotional security became attached to your ability to please others.** When excessive people-pleasing continues in adulthood, it can be less about bringing happiness to others and more about your needing to feel secure and loved.

People-pleasing can show up in different ways:

- Ignoring your personal limits
- Downplaying your point of view to appease others
- Disregarding your needs while elevating the needs of others
- Doing things you really don't want to do
- Giving with the goal of being liked
- Apologizing when you didn't do anything wrong

Does this sound familiar? If so, you might be in the habit of adapting your behavior to please others. People-pleasing is the blending of three codependent patterns: being unaware of what you need, having an identity based on interactions with others, and having weak personal boundaries. The more you tap into what you need, build stronger boundaries, and build an identity from within, the faster your people-pleasing behaviors will diminish.

*Coaching Exercise:*
*How to Say No to People-Pleasing Habits*

Practice these five steps to start saying no to people-pleasing habits.

**1. Why**. The next time you find yourself pleasing others, ask yourself, "Why am I doing this? Am I concerned others might be upset with me if I say no? Not like me?" Before you say yes, make sure your actions are aligned with your perspective and needs.

**2. Pause**. Instead of immediately saying yes next time you're asked to do something, say instead, "I'd like to think it over. I'll get back to you." This pause will help you move out of autopilot and give you some time to decide if you really want to do it.

**3. Reflect**. When you're asked to do something, ask yourself, "How stressful will this be? Do I have time for this? Will I have to give up something to do this? Am I doing this because I want this person to like me?" These questions will help you reflect on your motives.

**4. Flex**. Practice saying "no." The more you flex your "No muscle" the stronger it will become.

**5. Fun**. Have some fun by intentionally engaging in experiences that are the opposite of people-pleasing. This will help you get more comfortable with the disapproval of others. After a while, you'll begin to realize it's not as big a deal as you think. Here are some ideas: next time you're at a gathering with friends speak boldly about an issue you would typically be silent about, wear an outfit you would really love to wear but haven't because you're afraid, or do something you have been wanting to do but haven't because you were concerned about what others might think. Allow yourself to get out of your comfort zone. It's a fun way to get used to not always being on the receiving end of relational applause.

*Magic Habit 4.*
*Hold and Release Emotions*

Codependents are the kindest, most compassionate people you'll ever meet. They've been through a lot and understand what emotional pain feels like. They have tremendous empathy for others, but their empathy can also make them vulnerable to owning the emotions of others. There's a big difference between caring deeply and taking charge of another person's emotions. Caring deeply for another person means holding space for their pain but then releasing it back to them. Taking charge of another person's emotions means solving their problems, rescuing them from discomfort, and feeling their feelings way after the conversation is over.

**Be in charge of your emotions and let others be in charge of theirs.** This creates a healthy interaction, protects you from taking on more responsibility than you should, and prevents you from assuming the role of rescuer. It also creates a protective barrier between you and any toxic person who might try to make you feel responsible to change, fix, or rescue them.

One way to get out of the habit of owning other people's emotions is to acquire the skill of "hold and release." It's a method I teach my clients that helps to create sacred space for others and then release their emotions back to them.

Creating sacred space for another person is a wonderful way to provide support and concern. It's a great way to bathe others in empathy, love, and support without managing their emotions for them. Here's how to create sacred space for someone.

- **Define your role**. The best way to think about your role in a conversation is to imagine yourself walking alongside someone on a path. As you walk together, you're not pulling or pushing them forward, but simply walking alongside them, following their pace.

- **Clarify the goal**. This is the most important part of creating sacred space for someone. The goal is to provide unconditional support. Let go of any need to control, judge, fix, remedy, or rescue. It's not your job to manage the feelings of others or make their decisions for them.

- **Don't take their power away**. If you really want to create a sacred space for someone, you must provide support so they can make their own choices. Offer them love, encouragement, and guidance and release any tendency to take away their decision-making power. Give them the support they need to make their own decisions and mistakes. Permit them to trust their own voice and wisdom. Empower them.

- **Create a sacred atmosphere**. When you're walking alongside another in a conversation, make them feel safe by creating a non-judgmental, shame-free environment. As a space holder, your main job is to create an atmosphere that lets the other person work through their feelings. Be compassionate and empathic. Reflect what you're hearing them say. Affirm their point of view and experience. Validate their feelings. Offer strength and courage.

- **Hold Space**. When I create a sacred space for someone, I often generate an image in my mind. This image reminds me I can support others without feeling the pressure to be in charge of their emotions. I imagine gently holding their feelings in my cupped hands. I don't grasp them tightly in my fist. My intention is to provide a container for their feelings so they can feel safe enough to open up and work through their experience. Use this imagery to envision how to hold space for others.

- **Now Release**. This is critical. When the conversation is over, release their emotions back to them. It helps to imagine returning the emotions you are gently holding in your hands into their hands. Then imagine walking away. There's nothing more to do because you've already provided what they needed—sacred space. Imagery can be a powerful way to release the burden of feeling responsible for other people's feelings and problems. When you walk away, release control and responsibility. Tell yourself, "These feelings are not mine to own. I need to give them back to the person they belong to. It is not my responsibility to fix them, tame them, or resolve them."

When you create sacred space for somebody it also means allowing that person to make different decisions than you would make. Holding space for someone means releasing control and accepting differences. Learning how to hold and release emotions allows you to be supportive to others without the burden of feeling responsible.

*Magic Habit 5.*
*Build an Identity from the Inside Out*

It's natural to feel more confident when we receive the praise and approval of others. It can be quite satisfying to be needed. While this is a normal part of the human experience, if too much of our identity is derived from our interactions with others, our confidence can vacillate depending on our interactions. Instead, we need to build an identity based on deep awareness and appreciation of who we are.

The first step towards building an identity from within is knowing who you are. This takes time and a personal commitment to building self-awareness. The essence of this book is to teach you how to build the emotional muscles that will embolden you to tap into the power of owning your voice and being your true self. Building a strong identity is so important I have devoted all of Chapter 7 to the subject, "The Habit of Knowing Who You Are." Chapter 7 will provide the insights you need to discover who you are at the core and build self-confidence based on a deeper appreciation of who you are instead of what you can do for others.

## CHAPTER 3 IN A NUTSHELL

1. The habit of lowering your tolerance for crap is a pattern of setting healthy boundaries, and not tolerating toxic behavior.

2. Simply put, codependents seek out experiences that give them a feeling of being loved, valued, and needed. As adults, they repeat the patterns that worked for them in childhood: meeting the needs and expectations of others. Codependency comes from a silent wound of not feeling loved and secure.

3. Codependents are usually aware of what they feel but not aware of what they need. Asking for what they need is even harder.

4. The first habit of breaking free from codependent thinking is to become conscious of what you need and then respond to it. To do this, you will need to create a new lens that sees your needs are not less important than the needs of others and it's okay to include your needs into the decision-making process.

5. The second habit that will reverse codependency is to communicate your boundaries to others. Only you own that power. You are always teaching others how to interact with you, and this includes communicating what you are and are not okay with.

6. The third habit that will defeat codependency is to diminish people-pleasing tendencies. Excessive people-

pleasing in adulthood can be less about bringing happiness to others and more about needing to feel secure and loved.

7. The fourth habit that will help reverse codependency is not taking responsibility for other people's emotions. It's not your job. Instead, create a sacred space for them to share their emotions. Then let go of any need to control, judge, fix, remedy, or rescue.

8. The fifth habit that will help reverse codependency is to build an identity based on a deep appreciation for who you are at the core, not from interactions with others.

## QUESTIONS FOR GROUP OR SELF-REFLECTION

1. What are you tolerating that you shouldn't be?
2. Have you ever made excuses for another person's unacceptable behavior? If so, what advice would you give your past self now?
3. Have you ever adjusted your behavior in order to receive the love and approval of others?
4. What have you been needing that you haven't been willing to ask for?
5. Is there anything in your life that you need to say "no" to?
6. Have you ever found yourself owning another person's emotions? If so, what happened?

# CHAPTER 4
# THE HABIT OF EMBRACING YOUR INNER CHINGONA
## HOW TO BE ASSERTIVE AND CREATE MEANINGFUL TENSION

n Spanish, "chingona" is a derogatory word used to refer to a woman who is too assertive or bossy. I remember the very first time I was called a chingona. It made me feel ashamed and uncomfortable. I was fifteen years old and had started working at a local bakery after school. I was so excited about my new job. The only other job I had before it was working at our family feed store, Marquez Livestock Feed Supply. The feed store was a large, barn-like structure made of galvanized steel; it was situated across the driveway from our family home in Española, New Mexico. My siblings and I were required to take turns tending the store and its customers after school starting at the age of ten. My dad always believed I was capable, and therefore he provided opportunities where I could take initiative and wait on customers, take stock of inventory, order equipment, and manage the store in his absence. I had been working at the feed store for five years when I was offered the opportunity to work at the neighborhood bakery. I had to beg Dad to let me take the bakery job; it meant I would no longer be able to help with the family business. Additionally, I was not yet sixteen years old and needed his parental consent to work. I was elated when my father finally relented and granted permission—he'd let me if I was willing to save fifty percent of my paycheck.

I showed up at the bakery enthusiastic and determined to make a good impression on my boss, Miguel. My duties included keeping the pastry display stocked, waiting on customers, and cleaning up at the end of my shift. After my experience working at the feed store, I felt confident in my abilities and knew I would ace the job. On day five of my employment, Miguel stepped into the bakery to check in on me. I decided his visit was a great opportunity to impress him and started making recommendations on how to display the doughnuts so that they were more orderly and attractive. I also suggested we use plastic gloves when handling the doughnuts so that our hands would not be so sticky during financial transactions. Eager to make a good impression, I made a few more strategic suggestions I thought would be helpful. When I finished, my boss crossed his arms, and with disgust in his voice said to me, "Man, you're a chingona, aren't you?" He wasn't really asking me a question; he was making an accusation meant to make me feel small and ashamed for being too assertive. Instead of standing tall and embracing my inner chingona, I shrank like a violet beneath the scorching sun.

Looking back, I feel compassion for my fifteen-year-old

self. I was trying to take initiative and be a valuable employee, but instead of receiving encouragement for my behavior, I was told I was too bossy and overstepping. In my culture, I had offended his machismo. Events like this happened frequently throughout my youth. It is no wonder that for so many years, when I tried to be assertive, I felt I was doing something wrong.

Growing up, I received a constant litany of shame-inducing comments for being outspoken and strong-minded. In middle school I was reprimanded by a female teacher for raising my hand too many times in class and told, I should "give others a chance to respond." My first boyfriend told me I was too independent and recommended I be more submissive instead. When I was in high school, I initiated a conversation with the principal about the need to fund more scholarships for women applying to college. His advice to me was, "You would do much better in life if you would just learn how to rein it in and not be so pushy." In addition to being called too pushy, too assertive, and too independent, I was also called a chingona, bitchy, bossy, and worse by those who believed my assertiveness was something I should be embarrassed about.

Have you ever been made to feel uncomfortable when you were merely assertive or expressing a strong opinion? Have you been stigmatized as bossy for taking initiative? You are not alone. These negative messages are often hurled at assertive women.

It can be hard for women to speak up and assert their voice if it means dealing with pushback and criticism. There's a good reason for this collective reluctance—historically, women have been shamed for these behaviors with derogatory language or demeaning punishments. Strong and assertive women frequently experience negative sentiment for the same behaviors that men are often praised for. However, empowered women are assertive and willing to manage the tension that can come from doing so. **Empowered women know there are times when they need to initiate meaningful tension: they need to invite conflict in order to create important change or protect something they value.**

In my culture, the term chingona is used to keep women in a nonassertive or submissive position. Conversely, when men were called chingon, the masculine equivalent to chingona, it is meant as a compliment. This disparity reveals that when men are assertive or dominant it is considered a good thing; men are complimented for their strength. Women, on the other hand, are often disparaged for the same collection of assertive behaviors. Has this pattern changed over the last thirty years? Sure. But not nearly enough. Women are still stigmatized for being bold and outspoken.

Wondering if the meaning of "chingona" has changed over the years, I recently looked up the definition in the online *Urban Dictionary*. I was shocked to read the following definition, particularly since the word chingona has historically been used as a derogatory term to describe women in a negative way:

A **chingona** is a woman who chooses to live life on her own terms. They are the rebels of the world, the hardcore, bad to the bones women who don't take nothing from no-one. She is unbothered and doesn't care what others think. She is independent and fierce. She raises her voice while others keep quiet. Although "Chingona" is a Spanish term, chingonas come in all colors and cultures.[1]

In other words, in today's usage, a chingona is a woman who has ditched gender expectations of women and carved out her own path. She understands that being bold is healthy and empowering. She knows there are times when she needs to assert her perspective and initiate meaningful tension. She is more invested in being her true self instead of invested in being likable.

I have good news for women of every color. The Latina community is taking back the word chingona and using it as a term of empowerment—much like how women across the continent have taken back the word "bossy," a word which has historically been used to chastise women for being too tough, nonconformist, intimidating, assertive, or outspoken. Chingona is the Latina's equivalent of "bossy." However, now when we call each other a chingona, it is meant as a compliment to a woman's strength. Using this word, Latinas are collectively redefining underlying attitudes towards women who are independent and fierce. That's good news for all of us!

I no longer attach shame to being strong, nonconformist, bossy, or assertive. Instead of apologizing for these behaviors, I have learned to embrace them, now knowing they are healthy and empowering. I have learned they are desirable qualities that can help me amplify my voice and perspective. I have embraced my inner chingona!

Here are some qualities of Chingona women:

- Chingona women have learned how to break free from any gender expectations regarding what it means to be assertive.
- Chingona women have released any shame or discomfort associated with being assertive, strong, or any other way of being bold.
- Chingona women are willing to create necessary conflict and know how to manage the tension that may come from doing so.
- Chingona women are willing to speak up and let their voices be heard.

My story about working at the bakery and feeling "put in my place" for taking initiative is the story of women across the globe. As women, we have been collecting personal stories that have led us to believe that being bossy or a chingona is something to be uncomfortable with. But we shouldn't be uncomfortable. It's okay to be outspoken and let your voice be heard. Being able to assert your perspective works in tandem with living an empowered life. Assertive habits work hand in hand with many other habits mentioned in this book, such as getting out of your comfort zone (Chapter 2, "The Habit of Taking More Risks") communicating what you will and will not tolerate (Chapter

3, "The Habit of Lowering Your Tolerance for Crap") owning your authority (Chapter 6, "The Habit of Taking Up Space"), and more!

If you're ready to embrace your inner chingona, this chapter will show you how to break free from gender expectations and stand tall when you assert your perspective.

The first step is to accept that it's okay to be assertive and let your voice be heard. However, there will be times when being assertive means creating tension. When this happens, it's important not to take it personally. Tension is not necessarily a bad thing, especially when it's created to promote important change. I provide insights that will empower you to manage the tension that can occur when you are candid and how to work through any fear that can come from doing so.

The second step is learning how to weather criticism for being assertive. There are gender expectations that make it more difficult for women to be comfortable with expressing a strong opinion. Because of this gender bias, women are punished all the time for being dominant and forthright and face more pushback and criticism than men for these same behaviors. As a result, women often experience discomfort for behaviors that are healthy and empowering. I share research that reveals how women are stigmatized for these traits and how we can begin to change this cultural bias. Additionally, I provide five valuable insights that help women break free from any guilt or shame associated with being assertive.

The third step is learning when to create meaningful

tension. This section helps you understand how identifying your values can strengthen your determination to stand up for the things that are important to you. You will discover how a "value scale" can create the clarity you need to understand why creating tension can be necessary to protect something you value.

The fourth step is developing the habit of assertiveness. Diplomatic assertiveness is a powerful method that can be used to effectively share your voice. I reveal the three elements of diplomatic assertiveness: a softened start-up, a request, and a commanding posture. These three elements will give you the power to outsmart society's unconscious social bias toward assertive women.

Are you ready to embrace your inner chingona? If so, you are in the company of a legion of women who are ready to assert their voice without apology. **Toss out any traditional ideas that say women should be demure, quiet, or passive. Break free from these gender stereotypes. Instead, be a chingona and amplify the power of your perspective.**

## ACCEPT THAT IT'S OKAY TO BE ASSERTIVE

The first element of embracing your inner chingona is to accept that it's okay to be assertive and speak up. There is no good fundamental reason for being uncomfortable with these behaviors. However, there will be times when being assertive means creating tension, such as friction in a relationship or the discomfort of being stigmatized as bossy. When this happens, it's important to remember that just because you created a little (or a lot) of tension doesn't mean you've done something wrong.

When a woman is criticized for being assertive, over time she may begin to believe she is doing something wrong when she speaks up, sets boundaries, gets angry, or otherwise creates a ruckus. However, at some point, every woman will need to assert her perspective and create tension to protect something she values.

In my practice, I see fear creep up on women all the time when they imagine standing up for their point of view, especially when it means dealing with opposition. They tell me they want to confront issues that bother them, be included in the decision-making process, lead others, change policies, and more! They also tell me they fear being stigmatized as "bossy," or feel uncomfortable when they rock the boat. I get it; no one likes being labeled. It can cause us to talk ourselves out of being forthright. However, every woman has the power within her to assert her voice and manage any fear that might come from doing so.

Start by laying down a foundation of beliefs regarding why it's important to be an assertive woman.

- Your values and beliefs are worthy of assertion. What you have to say matters. Speaking up means you believe your voice needs to be a part of the equation.
- Sometimes you need to assert your voice to protect something you value or promote important change. I call this "meaningful tension." Tension can be a good thing when it leads to necessary change.

- Give yourself permission to be bossy or a chingona. There is nothing wrong with being a badass woman who is not afraid to speak her mind. Ditch the gender expectations and follow your own path. Live for your own approval and embody the confidence of a woman who owns what she believes.

Next, identify any fear or belief that might keep you from expressing a strong opinion and then challenge these beliefs. Naming the beliefs that hold you back can help lessen the power they have over you. Here are some of the most prevalent concerns I see women grapple with when they think about being assertive.

- People will think I am a bitch.
- I feel guilty when I cause tension.
- I want people to like me.
- I don't want to upset others.
- I don't want to hurt anybody's feelings.
- Does what I have to say really matter?

Do these fears and beliefs resonate with you? If so, they might be keeping you from elevating your beliefs and opinions. I understand. I too have struggled with several of these inner dialogues. However, they don't have to get in our way. We can challenge the beliefs that keep us from moving into action. The following coaching exercise will help you strengthen your resolve to be assertive even when it's difficult.

*A Coaching Moment:*
*Build Your Resolve to Speak Up*

If you are having trouble being assertive, reflect on the following coaching questions. They will help you build resolve and determination to speak up regarding issues that matter to you.

1. First, identify your fears. Pick from the list above or choose your own.

2. Second, imagine your fear materializes. The truth is your fear may be an accurate description of the opposition you face as a result of being assertive. As I mentioned earlier, society makes it harder for women to be forthright. For example, imagine your teammate refers to you as a bitch after you insist meetings should end on time. Aside from being uncomfortable, what is the worst thing about having to live through your fear?

3. What are three words of advice you can give yourself that will help you manage the discomfort you may feel as a result of being assertive? For example, "It's worth it because your beliefs are worthy of assertion."

Identifying the fears keeping you from stating your beliefs will help build your resolve to speak up even if it's difficult. You are stronger than you think. Don't underestimate yourself. You already have all the inner resources you need to work through fear. You just need to tap into them. It might not be easy rocking the boat, but sometimes it's necessary and often it's worth it!

## HOW TO WEATHER CRITICISM FOR ASSERTIVE BEHAVIOR

I am no longer surprised when women face pushback for asserting their voice. It's a common pattern in our society. It's sexism. One of my friends who is a pastor at a local church was told she should not be teaching men and should have never been given a role of leadership in the church. Another client, who is a stay-at-home mom, was reprimanded by her mother-in-law for insisting her husband share his decision-making regarding household finances with her. Another client was told by her boss she was being too self-serving when she asked for a raise and sought a more competitive position. These are not uncommon stories. Women are regularly criticized for assertive behavior, behavior that is healthy and empowering.

Women live with a Catch-22: we want to be seen and heard, but we may avoid doing so if it means dealing with social criticism. Women face a dilemma. On the one hand, we want to have our perspective be part of the conversation. On the other hand, we then must deal with being stigmatized as bossy.

The problem does not lie in the behavior of strong-willed women, but rather, with a society that expects women to align with more conventional aspects of femininity such as humility, modesty, and passivity. **We need to change this gender bias by changing our own bias; that is, we need to embrace the idea that there is nothing fundamentally wrong with being forthright**. We need to be outspoken without apologizing or feeling guilty. We need to hone our assertiveness skills and be unhesitant when speaking up. We need to be willing to manage the tension that may arise from doing so. When we collectively become more assertive and accept that doing so is healthy behavior, we can reduce the shame-based attitudes forced upon women and create a new normal. We can be the change.

You might be thinking, "Great! How do we do that?" Change starts by understanding both the subtle and direct negative social consequences women face for being outspoken and how these social consequences occur. Understanding these negative consequences can help us outsmart them. Research has shed light on how women are socially punished for being assertive. Research also shows that men usually don't have to manage this tension because they are more likely to be rewarded for being assertive. No wonder men find it easier to be forthright and women find it more difficult.

A research study led by David Maxwell and Joseph Grenny, sponsored by Vital Smarts (a leadership training company that focuses on researching human behavior and the written and unwritten rules that shape organizational culture), revealed that assertive women are judged more harshly in the workplace by their peers than men are, and this social judgment has an impact on their income.[2] In their study, which included 11,000 participants, they found when women's workplace peers perceived them as forceful or outspoken, their perceived competency dropped by a whopping thirty-five percent and their compensation dropped by an average of $15,088. Assertive men were punished at much lower rates and with less of an impact on their income. Finally, according to their research, both women and men were biased towards assertive women.

Another research study reveals the language used to criticize and describe "bossy women." In *The Abrasiveness Trap: High Achieving Men and Women are Described Differently,* researcher Kieran Snyder reveals how women are given gender-specific feedback on how to conform to gender expectations in the workplace and states the specific language used to describe women who were perceived as abrasive or too assertive.[3] In her research, which included the analysis of hundreds of reviews given to employees by their employers, Snyder noted that when women were perceived as abrasive or bossy, they were more likely to be given negative criticisms, such as "watch your tone," "step back," "you're being pushy," and "don't be so judgmental." For example, in one review, a female employee was told, "Your peers sometimes feel you don't leave enough room. Sometimes you need to step back to let others shine."

Her study also showed the word "abrasive" was used 17 times to describe 13 different women. For example, one woman was told, "You can come across as abrasive sometimes. I know you don't mean to, but you need to pay attention to your tone."

In other words, her research revealed women who were measured to be too bossy by their peers in the workplace setting were stigmatized and given critical feedback for this behavior. Instead of being affirmed by their peers for their authority and initiative, women were labeled with negative language and chastised.

Her research also revealed that the gender of the person giving the gender-specific feedback was not a factor; that is, both men and women tended to be more critical of bossy women and more likely to stigmatize them for this behavior.

**These studies confirm what women have known for years: women are judged more harshly than men when they are outspoken.** Therefore, it is riskier for women to speak up. Women are still expected to conform to cultural stereotypes such as being gentle and nurturing, and speaking forcefully violates these cultural expectations. Terms like "bossy," "abrasive," and "aggressive" are used to punish women when they are assertive. Whether this gender bias is conscious or not, it's important to acknowledge the result of the bias is part of our reality. Society does indeed make it harder for women to have a strong opinion and, because of that, we are at a cultural disadvantage. (Later in this chapter, I will address how diplomatic assertiveness can help women bypass this gender bias.) For now, here are five different approaches you can use to weather criticism when you are assertive.

*Five Tools to Weather Criticism*
*for Being Assertive*

**1. Affirmation**: Tension can feel uncomfortable. When you create tension by being assertive, give yourself some affirmation. Tell yourself, "It's okay to create a good ruckus in order to correct a negative status quo."

**2. Permission**: Give yourself (and other women) permission to be fierce without judgment. Embrace your inner chingona.

**3. Act**: Be more assertive. Even though it can be hard, remind yourself there is nothing fundamentally wrong with having a firm opinion.

**4. Commit**: Commit to using non-biased language to describe strong women (including yourself). Instead, use language that affirms this behavior as healthy and empowering. This will help reduce the shame-based attitudes forced upon assertive women—including yourself—and help create a new normal.

**5. Confront:** When you notice men or women using language that promotes gender bias against strong women, speak up. Say something like, "She's not being bossy, she is taking initiative." Doing so will help promote the cultural belief that it's okay for women to be assertive.

I will never forget a conversation I had with a mentor back in 1985 when I was twenty years old. My mentor, Karen Chew, told me frankly that I had two steep mountains to climb that others would not. Karen said that because I was a woman and also a woman of color, I would need to work ten times harder than my peers to compete for jobs, promotions, and acceptance into competitive institutions. Any other achievement I would pursue would be harder for me because I was Latina. At that time, there were not a lot of women of color in colleges, politics, corporate leadership, or any other positions of power. Oddly, I didn't feel resentment when I heard her words. Instead, I felt empowered because she armed me with an accurate description of the mountains I chose to climb.

Inequality is real. It's not all in your head, and it's not something that only happened to women in the past. It's a part of our current reality. But we can continue to outsmart gender bias by choosing to climb our mountains one step at a time. That's the power we have access to. Furthermore, it's important each of us helps clear the way for the women trailing behind us, just as there have been many women who have cleared the path ahead of us.

## KNOW WHEN IT IS WORTH IT TO CREATE MEANINGFUL TENSION

When I was a young girl, I used to collect the eggs from the chicken coop on our farm. I never liked doing this work because I knew entering the chicken coop would irritate the hens and create a ruckus. As soon as I opened the gate to the coop, the hens would begin to cluck loudly at me, peck at my feet in an attempt to make me leave, and fly from perch to perch causing their feathers to fly everywhere. But the ruckus was worth it. I would remind myself to work through the discomfort of literally "ruffling their feathers" not just because it was my job, but because I loved fresh eggs for breakfast. Being assertive is a lot like collecting eggs from a chicken coop—when you're about to ruffle feathers, it helps to know why it's worth it.

Creating a ruckus is another way to say, "asserting your perspective and causing meaningful tension." **Meaningful tension is conflict that we create in order to protect something we value or to create necessary change.** Tension can make us feel uncomfortable, even if we are creating it for a good reason. My clients often ask me how to determine when creating a conflict is worth it. They need to know how to tell whether the tension they are about to create is meaningful. I tell them it's worth it when something they value weighs more than the importance they place on maintaining harmony or likability.

I have a client named Anna (not her real name) who was perpetually bullied by her father. She found herself continually acquiescing to his demands and then ruminating over their interactions.

I asked her, "Why do you tolerate it?"

She said she didn't like it when her dad was disappointed in her.

I asked, "Do you feel disappointed in yourself afterward?"

Her face lit up. "Yes!" she said. "I feel so angry at myself! I wonder why I keep caving to his demands."

I asked Anna, "Do you believe *you* are worth not disappointing?"

Suddenly she sat taller in her chair. "I am! I am worth protecting! How I feel *does* matter."

We discussed her new awareness until she was clear on what she valued: she was worthy of protection and respect. She realized those two values (being protected and respected) were worth creating tension between her and her father. Clarifying the values that she wanted to defend strengthened her resolve to put up a fight the next time she was bullied. Identifying what she valued helped Anna remember why saying no to her father was worth more than maintaining constant harmony in their relationship.

When you're clear about the value you want to protect, you'll also be clear on why creating tension is worth it. Protecting what you value is the fuel for your fire. It will feed your willingness to make your thoughts count. It will remind you why your voice is a necessary part of the conversation.

The following coaching exercise uses a three-step process to help you discern when creating meaningful tension is necessary and worth it. Think about a particular situation in your life right now that you want to be emphatic about and change. Now, using this exercise, you can analyze the costs associated with being assertive and determine whether the change is worth the cost.

*A Coaching Moment:*
*When Creating Tension is Worth It*

### 1. Identify the cost of being assertive

Look back at the coaching exercise you just completed to

identify what you fear most about being assertive. Often, what you fear isn't real at all, but is something you're agonizing about that won't come to pass. Sometimes when your fear is real, what you fear is the *cost* of being assertive. For example, you might have to deal with relational tension. Undoubtedly, there are times when speaking up will mean saying yes to fallout. Here's a short list of the possible reasons you might be reticent.

- Your sister is disappointed in you after setting boundaries with her.
- Your husband becomes angry after you confront him about his gambling.
- Your mother-in-law criticizes a request to have her call before she stops by your home.
- Your coworker thinks you're abrasive after you confront gender discrimination in the workplace.

The cost of asserting your voice can be real. But sometimes, there are situations when it's worth being a little less likable. There are times when creating tension is worth the cost. If you are hesitant to assert your view, determining what the cost will be can help you understand the reason you feel that way. Understanding your feelings will provide the insight you need to decide if you want to take action. Start by identifying the potential cost of being assertive in your particular situation.

## 2. Identify what you value

Next, identify what you value. Conflict often arises when something we value is at stake. For example, I am a pretty easygoing person, but when someone responds to me in a sexist manner, I release my inner chingona and demand more respect. Knowing I place a high value on respect for women helps me understand why my normally calm self can quickly become feisty. Respect for women, myself included, is something I care deeply about. Therefore, I believe it's a value that is worth creating conflict over.

Identifying our values can help us determine when creating tension is worth it. Take a moment to think about yours. What do you care deeply about? What are the moral principles, beliefs, or virtues you want to protect? Why are these particular ideals meaningful to you? Naming the things you care deeply about will help to determine if they're worth protecting. Here are a few examples of values worth fighting for:

- Being heard
- Protecting someone you care about
- Protecting yourself
- Feeling respected
- Being treated with equality
- Pursuing justice
- Setting a boundary
- Asserting your needs

You might have a value that is not on this list. The

important thing is to name what you care deeply about because that value is the reason for a potential conflict.

### 3. Place the cost of being assertive and what you value on a scale

Imagine you have a scale in front of you. Using your response in Step 1, place the cost of being assertive on one side of the scale. Using your response in Step 2, place the value you want to defend on the other side of the scale. Now ask yourself: Which weighs more? The cost of being assertive or the value you want to defend?

Is your value worth protecting? Is it worth the ruckus? If so, why?

Using the imaginary scale in this coaching exercise helps you compare the weight of your decision and determine whether your ruckus is worth it. More importantly, it helps you understand *why* it's worth it.

## DEVELOP THE HABIT OF ASSERTIVENESS

At this point, you've decided why and when being assertive is worth it. You've confronted the underlying messages that made you feel guilty about it, and you've evaluated things like fear of social stigmatization and relational tension. You're ready to move into action to assert what you value or need.

I mentioned earlier there is an unconscious social bias towards strong-willed women. This bias has been proven by research and shows women are often punished for this behavior. Yet, according to this same research, there is a method that women (and men) can use to be forthright while side-stepping much of the criticism leveled at them. This method is called "diplomatic assertiveness." **Diplomatic assertiveness is a method of communicating that uses the skills of tact and conciliation combined with a firm and clear point of view.** Diplomacy helps bypass the stigma and bias towards forthright women. While there are many different methods one can use to assert their view, each having its own advantage, I have noticed diplomatic assertiveness works best in most settings. When women clothe their firm perspective with a conciliatory tone, it increases the likelihood of being heard.

Diplomatic assertiveness can be a powerful way to amplify your needs and perspectives without watering down your message. However, there are times when women literally need to raise the volume of their voice and be unapologetically aggressive! For example, I once had a man grab my ass in a Japanese subway. That was not a moment when I executed diplomatic assertiveness. Instead, I hollered at him, adamantly struck his hand off my body, and publicly embarrassed him. I have no regrets. It was necessary. The point is, it's going to be up to you to decide the level of assertiveness needed, depending on your situation.

Aside from those moments when you need to be bolder in your assertions, diplomatic assertiveness is a great tool to have in your toolbox and will help you effectively augment your perspective. Diplomatic assertiveness includes three elements: a softened start-up, a request, and a commanding posture. Each of these elements can add a diplomatic touch to your assertive style. Here's how to put these elements into practice.

*A Softened Start-Up:*
*The First Thirty Seconds Can Make All the Difference*

The first element of diplomatic assertiveness is knowing how to begin the conversation. According to psychologist and relationship expert John Gottman, the first thirty seconds of a conversation can often predict the remainder of the conversation.[4] John Gottman refers to this as a "softened start-up." In other words, if you carefully frame the first thirty seconds of a conversation with a respectful and disarming angle, you increase the likelihood you will be heard and that the recipient will remain open and non-defensive. Using a brief statement to frame your perspective at the start of a conversation can also reduce the social backlash women often experience when they assert themselves.

Below, I have listed several conversation starters that you can use depending on your situation. They will help you frame the first thirty seconds of a difficult conversation. Using them will help you be both assertive and diplomatic. **This method will help soften your pitch without softening your perspective.**

**For a personal relationship:**

- Here's what I want to talk about…
- Here's how I feel…
- Here's what I need…

**For a professional relationship:**

- Here's what I want to talk about…
- Here's my perspective on it…
- I believe this is a reasonable solution because…
- Here's how I think we should move forward…

These conversation starters may seem simple, but they work. Prepare these starters for yourself beforehand. Doing so will help you clarify your perspective and massage your delivery. I recommend putting these starters in your phone's note-taking application so they are easily accessible when you need to add a diplomatic touch to your assertive style.

*A Request:*
*What Are You Asking For?*

The second element of diplomatic assertiveness is making a request. When you're asserting your perspective, most likely you're doing so because you want to promote change— this might be creating a healthier relationship, more opportunities at the workplace, political change, and so forth. You are more likely to have a better outcome if you describe the changes you hope will occur as a result of being assertive. So, before speaking up, get clear on what you're asking for. You can do this by asking yourself, "What am I wanting/needing/requesting in this situation?" Then describe (to yourself) what you think the best outcome would be. This will help you articulate what you hope will change and increase the likelihood of a better outcome.

I worked with a client named Celina (not her real name) who was a youth minister at a church. She worked with a team of six men and was the only woman on the entire church staff. Her team was responsible for creating weekly sermons, orchestrating events, and mentoring over a hundred adolescents in the church and community. Celina was frustrated because her all-male colleagues were frequently making executive decisions without her when they were at the gym, golfing, and participating in other events that excluded her. She was determined to be included in the decision-making process and decided to use diplomatic assertiveness to spotlight how she was excluded and promote change. Here's how Celina approached the situation with her team and asserted her perspective.

> Hey guys, I've noticed a lot of decisions are made for the team when you all are hanging out. While I understand there are times when some decisions need to be made spontaneously [softened start-up], as a member of the team, I should be included in the decision-making process [her value] and would like an opportunity to share my perspective. Would you all be willing to agree to hold off on decisions until we are all together and I can weigh in [request]?

Notice how Celina described the situation non-judgmentally and then requested what she thought would be a fair outcome. Combining diplomacy with assertiveness enabled Celina to amplify her point of view. She used a conciliatory tone while still being clear about her expectations. She framed her perspective using a softened start-up but never watered down her message. Later, Celina reported her male counterparts were much better at making sure she was included in the decision-making process.

*A Commanding Body Posture:*
*Invite Your Body into the Process of Being Assertive*

The third element of diplomatic assertiveness is a commanding body posture. **You create a commanding posture by controlling your body language during critical conversations and making sure it conveys confidence and authority.** When it comes to being assertive, body language matters a great deal! If your words are strong but your body says, "I don't believe in myself," you'll give your listeners conflicting messages. When you decide to assert your perspective, make sure to include a strong body posture in the process. A commanding body posture that conveys strength will yield greater results.

In Chapter 6 of this book, "The Habit of Taking Up Space," I provide detailed guidance on body language and how to use it to convey confidence and authority. There, you can learn in detail about using body language for diplomatic assertiveness. Here is a summary that shows how a commanding posture works in the context of diplomatic assertiveness.

Your body's gestures, posture, and expressions greatly influence how others perceive you. Your body language will speak for you before you even utter a word. It's essential to exude confident body language when you're asserting your perspective. Therefore, before you speak up, do what I call a "body check."

Here's how: Take note of your posture—make sure you are standing tall and not slouching. Hold your head high and raise your chin. Be the first person to extend a handshake. Be the first person to start the conversation. When a person is anxious, they often shuffle their feet, so make sure your feet stay firmly planted on the ground even if you do feel nervous (there's no need to indicate to others that's how you feel). When other people are speaking, don't multitask; listening to others can be as powerful as being listened to. Give firm eye contact and speak with a strong tone in your voice. Pull your shoulders back; this will help you look and feel more confident. Others are more likely to pay attention to your message and agree with you when your body is communicating that you believe in yourself. So, make sure your posture matches the power of your message and communicates, "My opinion matters."

Combining diplomacy with assertiveness is a powerful way to amplify your point of view. These three elements of diplomatic assertiveness—a softened start-up, a request, and a commanding posture—will help others hear you, especially those who aren't as receptive to it.

I believe that every woman has an inner chingona who is waiting to be released. Her inner chingona is fierce, knows what she believes, and is willing to initiate meaningful tension when necessary. She is willing to speak up and be heard, knowing that her perspective matters. When your inner chingona shows up, open the door and let her in.

## CHAPTER 4 IN A NUTSHELL

1. The habit of embracing your inner chingona is a pattern of being assertive and creating meaningful tension.

2. A chingona is a woman who has broken free from any gender expectations regarding what it means to be assertive and released any shame or discomfort associated with being forthright and strong. She is willing to create necessary conflict and knows how to manage the tension that may come from doing so. She is not afraid to speak her mind and make her voice heard. She is unapologetically fierce and strong.

3. As women, we have been collecting personal stories that have led us to believe that being bossy or a chingona is something to be ashamed of. But those beliefs are wrong. It's okay to be assertive and let your voice be heard. There is no good fundamental reason for being uncomfortable with these behaviors. In fact, these behaviors are healthy and empowering. They are desirable qualities that can help you amplify your voice and perspective. Embrace these qualities and your inner chingona!

4. It can be hard for women to speak up and assert their voice if it means dealing with pushback and criticism. There's a good reason for this collective reluctance—historically, women have been shamed for these behaviors and criticized

with derogatory language. Strong and assertive women frequently experience negative sentiment for the same behaviors men are often praised for.

5. Being a chingona requires working through the fear of being thought of as bitchy or bossy. One way to do this is to identify any fear or belief that might keep you from asserting your opinion and then challenge these beliefs so they have less power over you. For example, you might need to challenge the belief that it's not okay to upset others.

6. Empowered women know there are times when they need to create meaningful tension because they want to promote important change or protect something they value. They are willing to assert their perspective and manage the tension that can come from doing so.

7. Diplomatic assertiveness is one way to outsmart the unconscious gender bias towards strong and confident women. Diplomatic assertiveness includes three elements: a softened start-up, a request, and a commanding posture. A softened start-up is a quick sentence that begins the conversation with a conciliatory tone. A request is a description of what you hope will change. A commanding body posture is body language that conveys confidence, presence, and authority.

## QUESTION FOR GROUP OR SELF-REFLECTION

1. Name three of your values that are worth defending.
2. Have you ever been called bitchy or bossy as a result of asserting your perspective? If so, how did you react to this gender bias?
3. When was the last time you had to overcome a fear or belief in order to assert your perspective?
4. Talk about a time in your life when you spoke up to protect something you valued.
5. Describe your inner chingona.
6. How do you want to release your inner chingona this week?

# CHAPTER 5
# THE HABIT OF VULNERABILITY

## HOW TO COURAGEOUSLY REVEAL YOUR TRUE SELF

Most of us have had at least one experience that shapes our view of vulnerability. I remember one of mine. In fact, I remember the exact moment. I was fourteen years old and had just witnessed a horrific interaction between my mom and dad. At the time, my parents were living in New Mexico. One day, my father announced he had bought a ranch in Colorado without first talking to Mom about the decision. He wanted to eventually retire there and had taken a forceful step to guarantee it would happen. Mom was reasonably upset she had not been included in such an important decision that determined where she would live and retire, so she confronted Dad. Instead of responding with respect or understanding, he responded with verbal and physical aggression. My mom eventually surrendered and gave up her attempt to be heard. I was filled with fear and anguish as I helplessly watched my mother surrender to my father's brute aggression and control. As I watched my mother tumble to the ground, I remember saying to myself, "I will never rely on another person. No way. If this is what it means to be in a relationship, I would rather be alone." Witnessing my mother's pain and vulnerability shaped my view of myself, relationships, and what it meant to be vulnerable.

I love both of my parents, and telling my story is not about assigning blame to them. Rather, I'm telling you this story to show you the impact their relationship had on me, and how it informed my view of vulnerability. After watching them, I associated the feeling of being vulnerable with being weak and powerless.

I had not yet discovered there is a type of vulnerability that is empowering.

This pivotal moment defined the next ten years of my life. To avoid feeling vulnerable, I did things that made me feel less dependent on others and more self-reliant. I worked three jobs in order to move out of my parents' house as quickly as possible. I researched careers that would ensure financial independence. I wanted to be financially self-supporting because I believed marriage would make me too vulnerable, and I vowed never to marry. I began to develop emotional self-sufficiency instead of learning how to trust others. I never asked for help or reached out for support. In conversations, I encouraged others to talk about themselves so that I could avoid having to disclose things about myself.

When engaging with other people, I often presented a contrived and controlled image of myself, such as a "tough girl" and "good girl" image. Worse, my true self was so different from the fake images: I was highly sensitive and had a wild-hearted spirit. I rarely showed my true self, and when

I did it felt very uncomfortable. Because I hid who I was, I was often very lonely; I achieved independence but was without a community I could be authentic with. It's hard to build an authentic community when you're only showing parts of your true self and not allowing others to live life fully with you.

Because I associated vulnerability with being weak and helpless, I did not develop the habit of being vulnerable, which means having the courage to fully reveal who you are.

The problem is that we humans must be vulnerable in order to show up in the world as ourselves. **Showing up as yourself means to truly be who you are as a person, not an image of somebody you think you should be**. It means making sure your thoughts, words, and actions are an honest representation of who you are. It means being authentic.

The truth was, I did need other people—we all do. More importantly, to stop hiding who I was and start being authentic, I needed to be vulnerable. To truly show up as myself in the world, I needed to learn that being vulnerable didn't have to mean being helpless and weak.

I finally learned my lesson about vulnerability after a serendipitous meeting with a wonderful man named Frank. I was twenty years old when I was introduced to Frank by a mutual friend on our college campus. He was sweet, sexy, shy, and absolutely gorgeous! After six months of shameless flirting, Frank had still not asked me out on a date. So I took matters into my own hands and asked him out. It was a heroic moment when my fierce independence and feminist views shined. We ended up dating for three years.

Love and relationships seemed to be so easy for some

women, but they were complicated for me. I struggled with the tension between my desire for emotional independence and my desire to be close to Frank. Building a strong relationship with him meant having to learn to rely on him and trust him. It meant I had to find the courage to show up as my real self and allow myself to be seen. The hardest part was knowing there was no guarantee that letting my guard down would not end in pain and disappointment. Dating Frank became a season of necessary change.

As my relationship with Frank grew stronger, I began to question one of my deeply held beliefs: that being vulnerable and needing others would result in me being weak and powerless. Looking back, I don't think I was aware of how deeply I believed that vulnerability equaled weakness. Developing a healthy intimate relationship with Frank caused me to rethink my perception of vulnerability.

One day I realized that I couldn't imagine my life without Frank. I wanted to marry him. This might not seem like a problem, except if you recall, I had made a vow earlier in life never to marry. I had worked hard to become self-reliant and self-supporting. Suddenly, my "me" was becoming a "we." Considering marriage caused a few seismic shifts in my beliefs. These shifts changed my life for the better. Not just because they allowed me to connect more with Frank, but because they helped me connect with myself and others.

These are the beliefs that reshaped my views about vulnerability.

First, I realized I was stronger than I was giving myself credit for. By then, I was twenty-four years old, a grown woman with inner resources I could access to help manage the experience of vulnerability. I was no longer a fourteen-year-old without emotional resilience watching my father hurt my mother. If I were hurt as a result of being vulnerable, I was now a strong woman fully capable of handling it. I was strong enough to embrace the possibility of being hurt, abandoned, and disappointed. Yes, I had to trust Frank, but I also had to trust myself.

Second, I recognized that I had power over my decisions. I could choose whether or not to be vulnerable. Being vulnerable was not something that happened to me, it was something I could choose. This realization revolutionized how I thought about vulnerability. I realized I had a choice whether to be in a relationship with Frank or anybody else. I could also choose to accept everything that came with that decision.

Third, I began to own my story. I recognized how my history had shaped my views and the image I had of myself and how shame was keeping me from being vulnerable. Part of owning my story included finding some meaning and purpose from the difficult moments in my life. Looking back, I can see how my mother's vulnerability frightened me and made me want to avoid being vulnerable. I never wanted to experience the pain I saw my mother suffer. However, I could learn from my mother's experience and choose a different life. I had control over that. I could engage in personal relationships that were emotionally safe and where power was shared. I asked myself, "How can I give this painful memory some purpose and meaning?" Eventually, I was able to use the wisdom I had gained from this difficult moment to teach other women how to cultivate relationships where power is shared.

Fourth, I realized there is a type of vulnerability that is empowering. Empowering vulnerability is the kind a person courageously chooses, recognizing the possibility of risk, being hurt, or getting out of their comfort zone. They choose this vulnerability because they want to fully reveal who they are, build better connections, or accomplish something important to them.

Yes, I wanted to experience love and belonging. But finding the courage to reveal my true self in my relationship with Frank also taught me how to show up in the world as my authentic self all of the time, and not just with him. It became the precursor to feeling comfortable being myself and being seen in general. I let my guard down and took a chance —in all aspects of my life. I began to practice the habit of vulnerability and share my perspective in many areas of my life, both personally and professionally. I chose to be courageous instead of comfortable. **Hiding in the shadows is a comfortable place to be, but you can't leave your mark on the world when you are hiding from others**.

I learned that vulnerability can be an empowering experience when it leads to:

- Being open and honest about who we are at our core
- Challenging the fears that keep us hiding in the shadows
- Creating a deeper connection with others

- Stepping out of our comfort zone and doing things that lead to being seen and heard

Vulnerability can birth fear and discomfort, but it can also birth connection, creativity, celebration, achievement, and the confidence that comes from being accepted for who you are.

Do you have the courage to reveal your true self—and therefore allow yourself to be vulnerable? It can be hard, but worth it.

For many of us, revealing our true selves is difficult. However, once you allow yourself to be vulnerable, you can also be your authentic self. **Vulnerability works in tandem with authenticity**. **You can't have one without the other.** Authenticity is so important I have devoted an entire section to the topic in Chapter 7, "The Habit of Knowing Who You Are."

In this chapter, I help you understand how your past has influenced your current view of vulnerability. This will enable you to evaluate if your current view of vulnerability is still working for you and make revisions if necessary. Shame, the feeling that you are not good enough or there is something wrong with you, is a powerful emotion that can leave you feeling sheepish about revealing your true self. I provide several insights that help alleviate the feeling of shame so you can stand tall and let others see you. Recognizing how your past has shaped your views and self-image can strengthen your resolve to be vulnerable and self-accepting. I will go into great depth about how you can own your story and your past so you can live more fully in the present. Finally, I expand on the difference between the type of vulnerability that promotes helplessness and the type that is empowering. These insights will help you fully embrace the habit of vulnerability so that you can fully reveal who you are.

## WHAT WORKED IN THE PAST DOES NOT ALWAYS WORK IN THE PRESENT

Each of us develops emotional habits that function for specific seasons in our life. However, when a season is over, we forget to let the habits go. It's kind of like putting on a warm jacket during the cold winter season and forgetting to take it off when the warmth of summer arrives. For example, I developed the habit of extreme emotional independence during a difficult season in my life—from my teen years through college. As a result, I learned how to be resilient, self-sufficient, and self-reliant—all great habits that enabled me to achieve many goals. They served their function for a season in my life. But because I developed these habits to the extreme, they also prevented me from developing other essential habits, such as building relationships and revealing my true self.

Emotional habits are often shaped by our experiences. We unconsciously develop habits in order to adapt to different environments and experiences. When it comes to being vulnerable, most of my clients have had at least one experience that led them to believe vulnerability is not a good thing.

If the thought of being vulnerable makes you want to cringe, you probably have something in your past that makes you feel that way. It's helpful to understand what past events have shaped your point of view. The following questions will help you to reflect on your current view of vulnerability.

*A Coaching Moment:*
*What Has Shaped Your Beliefs About*
*Vulnerability?*

1. When you imagine being vulnerable with others, what feelings do you feel?

2. How do you think your history has shaped your current view of vulnerability?

3. Are you willing to show up as your true self in the world? How does your willingness to be vulnerable affect your ability to do that?

4. Are you willing or able to be vulnerable enough to form a deep connection with others? If not, what's holding you back?

After reflecting on your answers, do you think your current view of vulnerability is still working for you, or does it need to be modified?

We all have emotional habits that were shaped by our upbringing. Sometimes we learn to avoid being vulnerable because we need to protect ourselves from dangerous situations, such as abusive parents or partners. There are times in our lives when protecting ourselves is the wisest thing to do. However, if you no longer need such protection, ask yourself if the landscape is steady enough to let your guard down. Remember, what worked for you in the past might not work for you in the present.

## VULNERABILITY, SHAME, AND THE COURAGE TO BE PRESENT AS YOURSELF: THE GROUND-BREAKING RESEARCH OF BRENÉ BROWN

There is a connection between vulnerability and the ability to be present as ourselves. Nobody understands this connection better than Brené Brown, a research professor from the University of Houston and the author of six *New York Times* bestselling books. She has spent the past ten years studying vulnerability, courage, authenticity, and shame. In Brown's popular TED talk, "The Power of Vulnerability," she describes the connection between courage, vulnerability, and showing up as ourselves.[1] In her TED talk, she says, "The original definition of courage is from the Latin word 'cor,' which means heart, and it means to tell the story of who you are with your whole heart." According to Brown, vulnerability means "Having the courage to be imperfect" and "letting go of who you think you should be in order to be who we are."[2]

According to Brown's research, there was something that got in the way of connection: shame.[3] For Brown, **shame is "the fear there is something about me, that, if other people know it or see it, that I won't be worthy of connection."** Brown noticed that shame keeps people from allowing themselves to be seen, to be known and to be loved, and therefore from having deep connections with others. She points out that people who form deep connections also fully embrace vulnerability. People who embrace vulnerability believe that what makes them vulnerable also makes them beautiful: they accept themselves as they are. In this way, **vulnerability and self-acceptance work hand in hand**. Furthermore, people who embrace vulnerability don't consider being vulnerable as either comfortable on the one hand or excruciating on the other. They simply believe it is a necessary part of life. Their acceptance of vulnerability allows them to reveal more of who they are, connect with others, and take risks.

Brown's wisdom can seem overwhelming at first, like a huge pile of golden nuggets. Let me break it down for you because I don't want you to miss anything.

- Feelings of shame—or feeling that you aren't good enough—might be keeping you from being vulnerable.
- Vulnerability is required to embrace the entirety of who you are and share the story of who you are with your whole heart.
- Courageous people are willing to give up who they think should be in order to be who they authentically are.
- People with courage create connections as a result of being authentic.

I wish I had heard Brené Brown's TED talk when I was a young woman. She has brilliantly described how connecting authentically, showing up as ourselves, and living courageously are all interconnected. She explains how, in order to live courageously, we also need to quiet any shame that keeps us from embracing the power of vulnerability.

Shame is a powerful emotion that can keep us from being vulnerable. It can be hard to show our true selves when we don't believe we are good enough. Next, I will provide several insights and a coaching tool that will help you set aside any shame that might keep you from living more courageously.

## OWN YOUR STORY

I was at a networking meeting with other therapists when one of my colleagues revealed that his coach was encouraging him to share his personal story and incorporate it into his branding. My friend was a Christian who had lived through a very painful divorce. In response to his coach, my friend said, "I'm not sure I can do that. I'm a marriage counselor. Wouldn't sharing my divorce cause my clients to think less of my ability to provide effective marriage counseling?" Adding to his reservation was the knowledge that, in the field of psychotherapy, we are trained to be cautious about disclosing personal information to our clients. The intention behind this restriction is to create clear boundaries between ourselves and our clients by not imposing our emotional narratives onto them.

As I listened to my colleague, I sensed there was another reason that he was hesitant to talk about his divorce with his clients or in other public venues, such as on his blog or radio show. Telling his story meant experiencing the shame he still felt from having a failed marriage. To feel comfortable talking publicly about his divorce, he first needed **to own his story. He needed to recognize how his past shaped his views and self-perception, and work through the shame that was keeping him from being vulnerable and telling his story.** If he could find some meaning or purpose from the pain of going through a divorce, it would help him quiet the shame that was keeping him from greater self-acceptance. He needed to accept his divorce as part of the fabric of who he was now, including how his divorce informed his ability to be an incredible marriage counselor.

What about you? Have you owned your story? Owning your story is a powerful way to cultivate self-acceptance, quiet shame, and give meaning to the difficult moments in your life. Owning your story can move you from feeling embarrassed about the bad things that have happened to you and help you feel greater self-regard.

There are three essential elements to owning your story: understanding how your history has shaped your self-perception, working through any residual shame associated with your past that might keep you from being vulnerable, and giving your story meaning and purpose.

*Understand How Your History Has Shaped Your Self-Perception*

First, begin to understand how your history has shaped your self-perception—the image that you have of yourself. Gaining this understanding takes time. It also takes reflection and objectivity. It requires working through the feelings, meanings, and messages you've inherited from your past. While your past does influence who you are today, it need not define you. There is no shortcut in this process. You must put in the time and do the work. While books can provide insight, when it comes to understanding how your past has shaped you and your self-perception, nothing is as effective as working one-on-one with a counselor. A seasoned counselor can help you reflect on how your history informs who you are today. Find a counselor who can help you work through any shame from your past that is holding you back. Take these insights and use them to own your story.

*Stop Standing in the Shadow of Shame*

After you learn how your history has shaped the image that you have of yourself, discern if you are living with any residual shame that might keep you from being vulnerable. If you recall, shame is a negative self-perception that leaves you feeling like there is something wrong with you. It's hard to be open and unguarded with others when we perceive ourselves as being unworthy or less than those around us.

Shame is a fierce emotion that can be debilitating if left unchecked. It causes a person to have a negative evaluation of themselves and breeds feelings of inadequacy. Feelings of shame can take root if you were raised in a critical, hostile, unstable, or demeaning environment. Living in an unhealthy environment as an adult—for example, with a critical partner —can also create feelings of shame. It is important to understand if you are living with shame so that you can move out of its shadow. Moving out of the shadow of shame and into the light of self-acceptance will help you look at your past with the objectivity needed to own your story without feeling embarrassed about the pain you lived through.

The most powerful way to reduce the experience of shame is to talk about the experiences that have led you to feel that way. Brené Brown has a powerful metaphor that explains why talking about shame-producing experiences can help lessen their impact. She uses a brilliant analogy that describes the antidote to shame. She writes, "If you put shame in a Petri dish, it needs three things to grow exponentially: secrecy, silence, and judgment." However, she continues, if you take those things away, shame loses its power: "If you put the same amount of shame in a Petri dish and douse it with empathy, it can't survive."[4]

Don't feed feelings of shame with secrecy and judgment. Talk about them. Expose them. Saturate feelings of shame with empathy from yourself and others. Determine that you will not be silent about the things that cause you to feel less than others. Exposing your shame to empathy will help you reevaluate who you are without imposing judgment. Ignite your inner courage and talk with a counselor or a wise person you trust. Then you can take the next step towards quieting any shame that might be holding you back. This will go a long way toward helping you own your story, cultivate self-acceptance, and show up in the world as your true self without hesitation.

*Give your Story Meaning and Purpose*

Once you have a better understanding of how your history has shaped you, and you've reexamined your identity without the imprint of shame, you can give your life story redemptive power. This happens when you can find even a little bit of meaning and purpose from those moments in your life that once caused you to feel inadequate. Every story is redeemable and can be given some value. After providing over forty-five thousand hours of therapy, I have come to realize everybody has the ability to give some meaning and purpose to the difficulties they've experienced. Every story has redemption—including yours.

What does it look like to redeem our shameful experiences? Allow me to tell a small part of my story and share how I learned to give meaning and purpose to an experience that once created a deep feeling of unworthiness within me.

I grew up in a volatile environment. I experienced emotional and physical abuse in my home. I also experienced abuse at my grammar school and in my community. Although I grew up in a large family of nine, I felt alone in my effort to keep myself safe. I was a shy kid and never told anybody about what was happening to me. Honestly, it never occurred to me to tell anybody.

I can't remember why, but one day I finally found the courage to speak up. I told an adult I trusted, a teacher, about what was happening to me. I shared a lot of details—for example, that I was having difficulty concentrating because I couldn't get the image of my brother being beaten out of my head. I told her that I was worried some of the other students would notice I often had bruises and belt marks on my body and make fun of me—adding to my already existing shame. Lastly, I told her I was afraid to leave school every day because two boys in my class, bullies, would regularly corner me and beat me up. I remember feeling both shame and relief after I shared my story, and I anticipated positive changes in my life as a result.

After I shared my story with the teacher, I expected her to help me. Although I didn't know it then, by law, she should have. But in the end, after I spoke up about the abuse, the teacher didn't intervene on my behalf. Instead, she simply ignored me and the situation. She never brought it up again or asked how I was doing. Worse than that, she never confronted the two boys from her classroom who were regularly beating me, an intervention this teacher had the power—and responsibility—to initiate. After this teacher betrayed my trust, my feelings of loneliness, fear, and helplessness grew.

After the experience of sharing my abuse and being betrayed by the adult I trusted, I believed that it fell on my shoulders to protect myself. I'm not sure I was even conscious of it, but I began to develop a way of interacting with the world that made me feel safer. I learned how to read the emotions and behaviors of others so I could respond in a way that pleased them. I learned how to disarm others by being kind and emotionally responsive to their needs. I developed fierce independence so I would not have to rely on others. These emotional habits made me feel that I was not helpless.

I wish I had not experienced a life defined by chronic fear and anxiety. But I had no control over my upbringing. What I do have control over, now, is my reaction to those experiences. **I have worked to no longer be defined by others who ignored my value, worth, and dignity.** Instead, I have learned how to redeem a life permeated with violence and give my experiences purpose and meaning. How did I do this?

- I draw on these painful experiences to respond to others with empathy and a deep understanding of how they feel. For example, when I sit with women and listen to their stories of helplessness, I draw on my own experiences to relate. I let them know I understand and that they are not alone. I let them know there is hope.
- I use my story to encourage others by sharing how I moved from feeling helpless and alone to being empowered and connected. I do so by including my story in my writing—on my blog, in articles, and in this book—and when I give talks on podcasts, in workshops, and public lectures. It took a while to get comfortable telling my story, but I found the more I talked about my experiences, the less shame I felt about them. Telling our stories is a powerful way to loosen the grip of shame and redeem our experiences. **Telling the story of your childhood as an adult helps you to reprocess what happened to you from an adult perspective**. Sharing your story with other adults can often help them shed light on their own stories.
- As an adult, I use many of the same skills I learned as a young girl trying to protect herself. In fact, I think of these skills as gifts. For example, I am good at reading people's emotions and behaviors, and I

use these skills when counseling clients. I am good at making clients feel comfortable, safe, and accepted. When I take on a leadership position, I know how to read a room and modify my leadership style to lead more effectively.

With these strategies, I give my painful childhood story redemptive power. I use my story, along with the feelings, words, and yes, gifts, that evolved from my difficult life experiences to uplift others. **I am not suggesting in any way that it's okay to minimize pain and trauma.** What happened to me was terrible. I did not have control over it. I only have control over my life as an adult. And as an adult, I choose to redeem those terrible moments by giving them a redemptive purpose and meaning. Your painful stories can also have redemptive power.

The more you own your story and release the shame you are holding on to, the more you will be able to embrace the power of vulnerability. The following reflection questions will help you put into practice the three steps you just learned.

*A Coaching Moment:*
*How to Own Your Story*

It's time to take a step towards owning your story. These reflection questions will help you do so. I recommend using a journal to jot down your responses to the following questions.

1. The first step is to understand how your story has informed who you are today. Doing so will provide the

awareness you will need to look at your past through the lens of your adult self. Reflect on your upbringing, significant past relationships, and the moments in your life that shaped who you are today. Now select from your story just one thing from your past that has shaped who you are today.

2. How do you think this specific story from your past has shaped the image you have of yourself? Include both the positive and negative influences you are aware of.

3. Reflect on your response to the last question. Do you think this part of your story has created any feelings of shame or unworthiness? If this part of your story makes you feel shame, how does this influence how you think about yourself?

4. Are there any feelings of shame or unworthiness from your past that are keeping you from being vulnerable with others?

5. It's time to saturate these feelings of shame with empathy and compassion. Reflecting on your last answers, respond to any feelings of shame with kind words, compassion, and understanding. Imagine that a stranger had written the words: what would you say to comfort her? Now, say these comforting words to yourself—compassion can start with you. Showing compassion toward yourself will help you release any

feelings of shame associated with this part of your story.

6. Now that you have showered this difficult part of your story with compassion, it is time to give it meaning. What are the good qualities you developed because of this difficult time in your life? Permit yourself to sing your own praises. For example, did you become more resilient, appreciative, tenacious, or compassionate? Did you learn coping skills or habits? Be specific. What are the good qualities you developed despite your difficult situation?

Owning your story does not mean that your past no longer ignites painful memories or feelings. But it does mean that you are no longer defined by that distressing past. Hopefully, these insights have shed light on how your history has shaped your self-perception, your views, and helped you take steps towards releasing any residual shame associated with your past. Hopefully, you have been able to find some meaning and purpose in the difficult moments of your life. Continue to own your story so you can boldly and unapologetically show up in the world as your true self.

## BEWARE OF THE WRONG KIND OF VULNERABILITY

Not all vulnerability is good. Some vulnerability creates helplessness and unhealthy fear. This type of unhealthy vulnerability does not cultivate a courageous heart. So, how do you tell the difference?

I wish there were an easy answer, but life is complex, and any trite answer I could give you would fall short. However, I can provide powerful coaching questions to help you discern if your situation breeds the right kind of vulnerability. The coaching questions I provide below are targeted to a specific situation in your life in which you face the choice to become vulnerable. The questions will enable you to discern whether this specific situation lends itself to the healthy type of vulnerability that fosters strength and confidence or to the unhealthy type that can leave you powerless.

As you reflect on each of the following questions, listen to your voice and hear what it has to say regarding your particular situation. Trust your gut. Then add some objectivity to the discernment process by asking a close friend or confidante to answer these questions with you while considering your situation. A wise and honest friend can provide invaluable insight regarding whether your specific life circumstance is cultivating healthy versus unhealthy vulnerability.

*A Coaching Moment:*
*Assessing Vulnerability*
*in a Particular Situation*

1. When you think about being vulnerable in this particular situation, do you instinctively feel helpless or empowered?
2. Given what you've learned about the benefits of

vulnerability in this chapter, will being vulnerable in this situation bring more harm or good?

3. If your situation includes a relationship with another person, is that person safe, reliable, and trustworthy?

4. Are you prepared to handle any feelings of disappointment that could result from being vulnerable?

5. Have you consulted people you trust and asked their opinion about whether your situation is worth the risk of being vulnerable?

6. Is this a situation where you need to protect yourself or open yourself up to new possibilities? How can you tell?

Answering these questions will help you say no to the wrong kind of vulnerability—the kind that fosters helplessness—and say yes to the type of vulnerability that is empowering. **Empowering vulnerability gets you out of your comfort zone because you want to do something worthy, such as reveal your true self, build better connections with others, or accomplish something important to you.**

## EMBRACE THE RIGHT KIND OF VULNERABILITY

It's not easy to embrace vulnerability. But it's worth it. We love it, dislike it, resist it, and need it all at the same time. We must be vulnerable in order to be real and authentic. We also have to say yes to vulnerability when we say yes to big challenges, such as taking a risk in order to elevate our careers, build bigger social media platforms, or engage in similar endeavors that amplify our voice.

Back when I first met Frank in college, and I slowly learned how to be more vulnerable, I used those same emotional muscles to start taking risks in other areas of my life. I built a trustworthy group of friends, colleagues, and fellow creatives. I applied to graduate school. I moved across the country—a huge risk—and started my career as a psychotherapist in an unfamiliar city. I started my own business, gave a TEDx talk, became a keynote speaker, and published a book. **Each of these personal challenges required vulnerability.** Sometimes I failed and made the wrong choices. At times, I faced criticism. I continually fought against my own perfectionist tendencies. But letting my guard down and being vulnerable was worth it, because it led to achieving things I never imagined I could do.

There are many ways vulnerability can be empowering:

1.  It helps create a deeper connection with others.
2.  It promotes a sense of authenticity.
3.  It can lead to personal growth and change.
4.  It can promote a willingness to accomplish something that is important to you.

That is the type of vulnerability I want you to embrace— the type that helps you be authentic and leads to the amplification of your voice.

Like any other emotional habit, learning how to embrace

vulnerability takes time. The good news is each encounter with vulnerability will prepare you for the next encounter. Each time you work through the discomfort of letting your guard down, you will realize you're stronger than you think.

There are many ways to practice the habit of vulnerability. If you feel safe to do so, share something about yourself with others that you typically don't share. Say yes to something that gets you out of your comfort zone. Do something you have been putting off because you were afraid to fail. Share your perspective with people who have a different view than you. All of these behaviors will help you to tap into the many benefits of healthy vulnerability.

## CHAPTER 5 IN A NUTSHELL

1. The habit of being vulnerable is a pattern of courageously revealing your true self.

2. When it comes to being vulnerable, most of us have had at least one painful experience that led us to believe vulnerability is not a good thing. Instead of letting a painful past shape your view of vulnerability, choose to shape your own view of it.

3. It takes a lot of courage to be vulnerable enough to show up as your true self and allow others to see you. Showing up

as your true self means being authentic and not an image of somebody you think you should be.

4. Feelings of shame, or not feeling good enough, can keep you from allowing yourself to embrace the power of vulnerability and experience the many benefits that come with it.

5. There is a type of vulnerability that is empowering. Empowering vulnerability happens when a person courageously chooses the possibility of risk, being hurt, or getting out of their comfort zone because they want to fully reveal who they are, build better connections, or accomplish something important to them.

6. Beware of the wrong kind of vulnerability. Not all vulnerability is good. Avoid vulnerability that fosters helplessness, powerlessness, and unhealthy fear.

7. Own your story. This means understanding how your history has shaped your self-perception, then using this awareness to quiet any shame that is keeping you from being vulnerable. Part of that process includes finding some meaning and purpose in the difficult moments of your life.

## QUESTIONS FOR GROUP OR SELF REFLECTION

1. Describe a moment when you found the courage to

show up as your true self, even though it was difficult.

2. How has your story shaped your view of vulnerability?

3. Is your current view of vulnerability still working for you? Why or why not? Remember that what worked for you in the past might no longer work for you in the present.

4. Describe the difference between the type of vulnerability that is empowering versus the type of vulnerability that fosters helplessness. How have you experienced these types of vulnerabilities in your life?

5. When was the last time you chose to be vulnerable? What did you learn from this experience?

6. What have you been able to accomplish in your life because you were willing to share your thoughts, ideas, or feelings?

# CHAPTER 6

# THE HABIT OF TAKING UP SPACE
## HOW TO CLAIM A POSITION OF LEADERSHIP AND OWN YOUR AUTHORITY

When I was twenty-one years old, I turned down my first opportunity to take a big leadership role. I was spending the summer in Daytona Beach, Florida, with a faith-based group called Cru. I was there with sixty other college students on an annual, eight-week-long retreat to experience the meaning of community, grow closer to God, and learn how to see the world through God's eyes. Each summer, the senior Cru staff left mid-session and handed leadership over to a college student. If chosen to be the Cru leader, the student would assume authority over the other college students for the rest of the summer and provide complete oversight of the project. The leader's duties included mentoring students, managing the budget, team building, supporting each student in their spiritual growth, and more.

One day, John, one of the staff leaders from Cru, asked me to take a walk on the beach. I assumed the walk was simply an opportunity to get to know each other better. We were leisurely walking along the sand when John asked me a question I was not expecting.

"The Cru staff have been observing you all summer," he said, "and we would like you to take over leadership for the remainder of the summer after we depart. Are you willing to do this?"

Without breaking my stride I looked up at John and said, "I am so flattered, but not a chance! There is no way I can be the summer project leader."

Needless to say, John was caught off guard by my resistance to accept a position of leadership and asked about my reason why.

I meekly told John I believed the Cru staff had made a big mistake in choosing me, and that I was not the right person for the task.

Why did I tell him this? My inside voice was telling me I was not good enough, not capable, and not ready to step into a position of authority. I believed I was better suited for the sidelines. At that point in my life, I had no cultural or spiritual template of what a woman with power, authority, or visibility looked like, so I couldn't embrace being such a person.

Looking back, I now realize I had inherited several toxic messages from my upbringing in a Latin culture and the church. My life experiences led me to believe my value to society was less than that of my male counterparts—in large part because of my faith experience. As a woman of faith, I believed my role was to be small, silent, meek, and subservient. I believed a woman's place was on the sidelines. Throughout my childhood and teen years, I had heard numerous sermons directed at women stressing the importance of submission and passivity, the beauty of having a quiet spirit, and the value of obedience. No one in my church had ever taught me that, as a woman, I was also fully equipped to lead or assume authority. I remember being told women are not supposed to lead men, preach to men, or assume any position of authority over men. And these were just *some* of the heavy messages I was burdened with. Does any of this sound familiar? If you were raised in a certain type of church, then you probably heard similar messages, too.

During that walk on the beach, John from Cru seemed to accept my rejection of his leadership offer. However, my walk with him forced me to confront my view of women in leadership and challenge the image I had of myself. After all, if I weren't cut out for leadership, why would Cru have offered that role to me? After that conversation, I had to ask myself some hard questions: "Why aren't I fully capable of leading others?" "Is there a legitimate reason why I cannot embody authority over others?"

Thankfully, my story didn't end there. A few days later, John and I went on another walk on the beach.

"Margo," he said. "We still believe you are the best person to lead the team. I want to know why you can't see that. More than that, I'm willing to help you work through whatever is holding you back from claiming this leadership role."

His words changed my life. I eventually agreed to lead

Cru, even though I was scared and felt terribly inadequate. While leading Cru that summer, I realized that my fear was not indicative of my ability. I realized that I was fully capable of leading the group, using my perspective and unique style of feminine leadership.

Through my counseling practice, I have learned my story is the story of many women. Women often fear owning their power, authority, and influence. Some of this tension is born out of the messages we've internalized about what it means to be female and feminine, how one cannot be feminine and powerful at the same time. These messages are false, and we can change them.

One way to overcome any barrier that might keep you from stepping into a position of leadership is a habit I refer to as taking up space. **Taking up space means using your perspective, body language, and voice to claim a position of leadership and authority.**

There are many ways to practice the habit of taking up space, including being aware of our body language. However, taking up space requires more than just an outward shift of the body. As this list shows, taking up space requires an inward shift of the mind.

In my work as a psychotherapist, I have noticed that women are much more likely to struggle with taking up space than men. That's not a big surprise because historically women have held less power than men. When you have less power, it can be more difficult to be heard and seen. **However, when you take up space, you are claiming your inherent power to lead others.**

Silence has also been a part of the feminine inheritance.

Despite the rise of women in power and influence, women are still not seen as often as men in positions of leadership in politics, the church, entertainment, and business. Silence and powerlessness go hand in hand. Taking up space is the antidote to silence. We each possess the power to amplify our unspoken words into the world and lead others.

It's time to unleash that power. I will teach you how to take up space with your body, voice, and perspective. I will empower you to remove any self-doubt that keeps you from stepping into leadership or gaining visibility.

This chapter examines the four elements of taking up space that you can use to claim a position of leadership and authority. Taking up space includes:

- Learning how to own your perspective
- Learning how to manage any fear keeping you from stepping into leadership
- Learning how to use your body language to exude confidence
- Learning how to practice visibility

It's time for you to be heard and assert your power.

## OWN YOUR UNIQUE PERSPECTIVE

The first element of taking up space is owning your unique perspective on the world. **Owning your perspective starts with knowing who you are and believing in yourself**. If you don't know yourself and believe in yourself, others will pick up on it. When you walk into a room, you bring all of the beliefs you have about yourself with you. For example, if you don't feel confident, others will know. Therefore, it is important to understand who you are and become comfortable in your own skin. (In Chapter 7, "The Habit of Knowing Who You Are," I address in greater detail how to embrace your identity).

Taking up space also involves believing your perspective has value. Just before I gave a TEDx talk in 2017, I was backstage getting ready to go in front of the cameras, lights, and a live audience. I was going over my talk when I realized I had received a voicemail from my dear friend Tabby Biddle. I stopped preparing and listened to her voicemail. She shared several words of encouragement, but there was one thing she said that immediately became emblazoned on my psyche.

She said, "Margo, when you walk on stage, own your feminine authority."

*Own your feminine authority.* Those were very powerful words.

What do they mean?

**How to own your authority:**

- Own your unique way of sharing your story and message from your perspective.
- Own that you are the authority on the subject you are speaking about.
- Own your ability to lead in this moment.
- Own who you are.

My friend Tabby was asking me to believe my perspective

had value so that I could share it with authority. That belief was an essential element of being able to step onto the stage and take up space. I realized the more I embraced my own perspective, the more I would be able to deliver my ideas with authority. Conversely, if I was unable to embrace my perspective, how would I be able to convince others that what I had to share had value?

Tabby's words were a game-changer for me. In that moment, I realized nobody could give me the ability to own my unique perspective. Only I had the power to do that. And so I did. I walked on the stage willing to take up space and own my unique perspective on the subject of shame and how it affects how we think, feel, and interact with others—the topic of my TEDx talk.

Before that phone message from my friend, I had never been told to "own my authority" before. Have you? When I talk to my male friends, they tell me they have been storing up messages about the importance of male authority for years. Similarly, women need to store up messages about the importance of owning their authority and believing in their particular view of the world. The world needs the influence of your perspective; but first, you must clarify it.

*A Coaching Moment:*
*Clarify Your Perspective*

It takes time to clarify one's perspective. However, I have found the more time my clients spend reflecting on their unique viewpoints, the more willing they are to share them.

So, I have created a few writing prompts designed to help you own and develop yours.

1. What are you afraid to admit about yourself to others? For example, are you more liberal than your conservative peers? Describe your fear.

2. Is there anything you are lying to yourself about? If so, bring it out of hiding and write about it. After journaling about this question, ask yourself, "How can I own my perspective on this issue?"

3. Finish this sentence: "I am a woman who can…"

4. Finish this sentence: "If I had the opportunity to stand on a stage and share something with a crowd, the message I would share is…"

5. What makes you unique? Think about your traits, skills, abilities, and history.

Be intentional about gaining clarity on your unique perspective. You see the world through a lens that is as unique as a fingerprint—no two are exactly alike. Understanding the lens with which you view the world is one of the best investments you can ever make and will go a long way in helping you own your voice and use it.

Through the power of self-awareness and the support of some amazing coaches, I have learned a lot about my unique lens and how to use it to lead others. For example, I know what powerlessness feels like. I also know how good it feels to be empowered. I have learned that this knowledge adds fuel to my fire and emboldens me to push through my innate shyness so I can deliver my ideas with authority. Self-awareness can help us gain clarity on how we see the world and how we take up space.

Whether you are stepping onto a stage or walking into a room, you bring all the beliefs you have about yourself with you. So, it's important to understand who you are. It's important to understand any beliefs that could undermine your ability to lead and influence others. More than that, it's important to believe in yourself and your viewpoint. The more you invest in knowing who you are, the more you will be able to walk into a room with the presence of a self-assured woman.

## WHAT FEAR IS KEEPING YOU FROM STEPPING INTO LEADERSHIP?

Over the years, I have coached a lot of women; each wanted to amplify her voice and build her leadership presence. Clients tell me they want to have more influence and use their superpowers for good. They want to make a positive change in the world and build things that matter. To do that, they have to be comfortable with **being visible. That is, they need to be willing to come into the full view of others and promote their leadership style, ideas, and perspective.** Being visible entails working through the fears that keep them from stepping into leadership with confidence.

Inevitably, as my clients work on these goals, they begin to face some big fears about what it means to come into the full view of others and lead. When we start to talk about those fears, these are some of the words I hear:

- Am I capable of leading?
- I don't want to take up too much of the spotlight.
- I am afraid others will think I am showing off.
- What if I sound stupid?
- What if I fail?
- I'm not sure if my perspective has value.
- What if someone challenges my ideas or what I have to say?

Have you struggled with any of these doubts? If so, you are not alone. These doubts are rooted in the fear of stepping into leadership. It can be hard when others disagree with you or simply disregard your viewpoint. In addition to having these fears, women often practice massive self-judgment.

I get it. I've been there. I know how uncomfortable it can be to move from the shadows into visibility. I have had to work through my I-am-just-a-small-town-woman-of-color-from-nowhere-New-Mexico fears, and I've wondered why anybody would ever want to listen to what I have to say. I, too, have had to work through fears around visibility so that I could take up space with my thought leadership.

I soon learned that my fears were just that—fears. When you begin to take up space and move into visibility, you're going to feel uncomfortable. That's okay. It's a normal part of the process of growing into a person who owns their ability to lead.

When we begin to make the choice to be visible and move into leadership, it's normal for fear to creep in and tempt us to step back into the shadows. When that happens, it's helpful to have a few tools to get you through those uncomfortable moments. Fear can be very powerful, but there are many ways to manage it. For example, in Chapter 2, "The Habit of Taking More Risks," I share how to shift one's mindset from perfectionist thinking (a tendency to set personal standards that are so high they either cannot be met or met only with great difficulty) to the Good Enough Equation mindset. The Good Enough Equation mindset is the decision to set aside any belief that says you need to achieve your goals perfectly and instead to give yourself permission to be "good enough." Shifting from perfectionism to "good enough" is scary, so I also share how to tap into your existing inner resources to manage fear.

Let's add one more tool to your "how to kick fear in the butt" toolbox so you can step into leadership and feel more comfortable being visible. In addition to the shifts in thinking I just mentioned, you can also change how your brain is functioning to reduce the physical experience of fear and gain more control over how you're feeling. By shifting which part of your brain is in control, you can take over the driver's seat.

Here's how it works. Fear is both a mind and body experience. It exists in your thoughts ("I am going to fail and look like an idiot!") and in your body (heart racing, shallow breathing, fingers twitching, stomach churning, etc.). Shifts in thinking (for example, the Good Enough Equation) are great tools for calming the cognitive experience of fear. You can also shift which part of your brain is in charge and ease the physiological experience of fear. Let's take a look at how the brain and body handle fear together.

Not all fear feels the same. Sometimes fear is mild and sometimes, well…it just runs wild! When the experience of fear gets wild, physiological changes occur in the body: your heart rate increases, palms sweat, muscles tighten, and breathing becomes more rapid. Blood flow actually moves away from your heart and through your limbs and muscles, making it easier for your body to fight or run from the source of your fear. This is called the fight-or-flight response, and it's your body's way of protecting you from danger. The response doesn't care whether the source of your fear is a hungry mountain lion chasing you or an imminent talk you must deliver in front of a large audience. The body's response is the same.

Additionally, when fear moves from mild to wild, stress hormones like cortisol and adrenaline course through the body and activate a region of the brain called the amygdala, placing the amygdala in the driver's seat of your mind. The amygdala diminishes decision-making ability and increases fear. You could say the amygdala essentially hijacks the frontal cortex (which is the logical, problem-solving part of the brain), making it harder to think clearly. As long as the amygdala is in control, fear will run rampant in your brain *and* body. Your goal is to get the amygdala out of the driver's seat and into the back seat where it doesn't have control. Then, put the logical frontal cortex in the driver's seat to calm things down.

You're probably wondering, "How do I control which part of my brain is in the driver's seat?" Here's the answer: deep breathing. By engaging in long, deep, deliberate rhythmic breathing, you can shift which region of your brain is in control and lessen the experience of fear.

Here's why. Deep breathing triggers a series of physical reactions in the body. While it increases the supply of oxygen to the brain, it stimulates the parasympathetic nervous system, promoting a state of calm. Deep breathing slows down your heart rate, which helps move the body out of the fight-or-flight response. Deep breathing also helps relax muscles in the body and soothe other physical sensations of fear, such as an upset stomach, trembling, and sweating. Changing your pattern of breathing can help you control which part of your brain is in your body's driver's seat and return you to a state of calm.

*A Coaching Moment:*
*How to Use Deep Breathing*
*to Reduce the Feeling of Fear*

Let me give you a play-by-play of how to use deep breathing to reduce fear the next time it creeps up.

1. Notice the intensity of the fear you are experiencing. Ask yourself, "How would I rate my fear right now on a scale of one to ten? Give the intensity of fear a number on a scale of 1 (Mild) to 10 (Wild).

2. Notice the physical sensation of fear and how it's showing up in your body. Below, I've provided a list of some of the most common ways the body reacts when

fear skyrockets. Circle the one(s) that best describe your physical experience of fear.

Rapid heartbeat | Upset stomach
Nausea | Rapid thoughts | Trembling | Dry mouth
Sweating | Fingers twitching | Shallow breathing
Nervousness

3. Next, take note of whether your breathing is shallow or rapid. Then close your eyes and begin to concentrate on your breathing. Let yourself settle. Try the following:

- Begin to breathe in through your nose and out through your mouth, inhaling slowly and exhaling slowly.
- Notice the rise of your chest as you inhale through the nose. Notice the lowering of your chest as you exhale through the mouth.
- As you breathe, try to imagine the oxygen flowing throughout your body, relaxing the muscles in your neck, face, and jaw.
- Imagine your spine lengthening toward the sky as you take a deep breath in.
- Feel your shoulders softening down as you exhale.
- Take five deep breaths in this fashion, counting to five as you inhale, and counting to five as you exhale. Five deep breaths in, five deep breaths out.
- Take a moment to notice the quietness of your mind and the stillness of your body.

- Slowly open your eyes and bring your awareness back to your surroundings.
- Take a moment to notice how you feel. Do you feel calmer and less fearful?

4. When you're finished with the deep-breathing exercise, notice how your body is calmer and more relaxed. Then ask yourself, "How would I rate my level of fear on a scale of one to ten? Give the intensity of fear a number on a scale of 1 (Mild) to 10 (Wild).

This is a simple breathing method, but it isn't superficial. It works! You can diminish the emotional and physical experience of fear by changing the way you breathe. Deep breathing is a powerful tool that can be used for managing any fear that might be keeping you from stepping into leadership.

You have something of great value to bring into the world —you! Don't wait any longer to do that. It's time to have influence and use your superpowers for good. Don't let fear keep you from standing in the spotlight. Instead, use these tools to work through any fear that might be keeping you from gaining visibility and taking up space.

## OUR BODY LANGUAGE HAS A LOT TO DO WITH HOW WE TAKE UP SPACE

So far, I've shared two elements of taking up space: how knowing who you are can help you own your perspective and learning how to manage the fear that keeps you from stepping into leadership. These first two elements address how to make inward shifts of the mind that will empower you to take up space. The third element addresses how an outward shift of the body can help you take up space.

When it comes to taking up space, body language matters a great deal! When you walk into a room, your body language can radiate confidence, or it can exude insecurity. Your body language will reveal your inner attitude before you ever speak a single word.

For example: If I am at a networking meeting and my shoulders are hunched, my gaze is sheepish, and I mumble during conversations and then tell my colleagues I'm a really good public speaker, chances are they won't believe me. That's because my body is communicating a lack of confidence and presence, two qualities required of good public speakers. However, if instead I stand tall with my shoulders back, give steady eye contact, and initiate a conversation with a bold and unwavering tone, then my colleagues are much more likely to believe me when I tell them I'm a good public speaker. When it comes to communicating who we are and what we believe about ourselves, body language counts. Our body language can convey, "I believe I am fully capable of leading, and my perspective has value." It can also convey, "I don't believe I am a leader, and my perspective is not worth asserting."

Your body's gestures, posture, and expressions influence how others perceive you. **Your body tells others how to relate to you before they ever hear your voice.** So, when you need to take up space, first do what I call a "body check." Before you enter a room, get on stage, speak to your boss, or engage in any important conversation, make sure your body exudes confidence and authority. You can do a body check by noticing what your body is communicating. Make sure it is saying, "I am confident, capable, and strong!"

**How to do a body check:**

- Stand tall with your shoulders back.
- Uncross your arms.
- If you are standing, make sure your feet are firmly planted. Don't cross or bend your legs.
- If you're sitting, sit up straight and raise your chest.
- When you are interacting with others, don't multitask. Give the other person your full attention.
- Don't fidget; fidgeting can convey nervousness or anxiety.
- When greeting others, give a firm handshake.
- If you have a quiet voice, increase the volume enough so that others can hear you.
- Use unwavering and focused eye contact to command attention. Don't be sheepish with your gaze.

These empowering behaviors will not only influence how others perceive you but will also influence how you feel about yourself. Research shows that simple changes, such as sitting up straight in a chair, can significantly change how you think about yourself.[1] Researchers from Ohio University gathered 71 college students, split them into two groups, and had each group engage in two different body postures. Half of the students were asked to slouch in their chairs and look at their knees during a task. The other half were asked to sit up straight and push out their chests. Afterward, each student was asked to rate themselves. The students who were told to sit up straight and raise their chests rated themselves as having more confidence than the students who were asked to slouch and face downward.

Similar results were found in another study on body language by Amy Cuddy, a social psychologist and Harvard professor.[2] She and her research team found that structuring your body into "high-power postures," such as standing tall with your shoulders back and fists anchored on your hips (the "Wonder Woman pose"), for as little as two minutes increases testosterone, the hormone linked to power and dominance, and lowers levels of cortisol, the stress hormone. In other words, body behavior can literally affect our brains, making it easier to take up space with our bodies.

What I'm describing are power poses, and they are great tools for feeling confident fast. **A power pose is physically standing or sitting in an open or expansive stance to increase a feeling of confidence.** It's a powerful method that you can use to amplify your presence and exude confidence by using body language. In Chapter 8, "The Habit of Listening to Your Body's Voice," I provide a step-by-step sequence of examples: The Wonder Woman and Victory Woman power poses.

Your body language helps determine how others perceive you. **Get into the habit of being aware of what your body is communicating to others.** Take note of your gestures, posture, facial expressions, and tone of your voice. Does your body posture say, "I am sorry I'm here?" Or does it say, "I am here, and I am a force to be reckoned with?" Be aware that your body is communicating with others all the time. You have the power to exude confidence by taking control of what your body language is communicating. The world needs the influence of your unique perspective; knowing how to radiate assertive body language will empower you to exude the presence of a powerful leader.

## PRACTICE VISIBILITY AND EXERCISE YOUR AUTHORITY

The fourth element of taking up space is practicing visibility, the act of intentionally being seen and heard. **Practicing visibility means finding ways to promote your leadership style, ideas, and perspective.**

**Why is visibility important?**

- Practicing visibility builds your confidence and ownership of your perspective.
- Practicing visibility helps you work through the fear of being judged and criticized.
- Practicing visibility is a powerful way to claim your authority and lead.
- Practicing visibility is an action that announces that what you have to say matters.

Earlier, I shared a story about the time I was twenty-one years old and initially rejected an invitation to lead sixty college students during an eight-week summer program. Eventually I said yes, even though I was terrified, felt inadequate, and was uncertain how to lead the team from my unique perspective. Despite my self-doubt and fears, I somehow found the courage to move into action and say "yes" to being seen and heard. That's an example of how to take steps towards visibility. During most of that summer, I struggled with fear and self-doubt. In fact, I never did feel confident in what I was doing until the last few days of the program. Each day, I made the best decisions I could, leaned into my instincts, and worked through each moment of self-doubt. Looking back, I now realize I was doing a fine job as a leader and had no real reason for self-doubt. Thankfully, **feeling confident is not a requirement for stepping into leadership.** Being willing to say "yes" to being seen and heard was the requirement for me that summer. I had to be willing to move out of the shadows and into the light while I was still struggling with fear and self-doubt. Only then could I cultivate my unique style of leadership.

It's okay to say yes to opportunities that will allow you to share your voice, even though you're unsure of yourself. Practicing visibility will help you work through the fear of being judged or criticized. Trust that you have the inner resources to figure it out. Surround yourself with others who believe in you and can provide the coaching support you need to develop your perspective and abilities. Over time, you will gain more clarity about who you are, build more confidence, and develop your leadership style. Just say yes. Then trust the process, and yourself.

*Promote Your Leadership Ideas*
*on a Small Scale*

The best way to learn how to embrace visibility is to start with small actionable steps. I call these "little habits." Remember, what you practice grows stronger. So, start with changing little habits first. Look for opportunities to ease into sharing your perspective. If you do this, over time you will become more comfortable with visibility on a larger scale.

I am naturally shy and extremely introverted, so, for me, moving into visibility has been hard. However, the more I practiced, the easier it got. Before I became comfortable with sharing my perspective through podcasts, radio, and public speaking, I started with smaller steps, such as speaking up in conversations. For example, I would share my thoughts on the role of women in the church in conservative circles. This helped me own my perspective and accept that not everybody would agree with my view. I talked about why the gender parity gap in our church is problematic and why teaching women empowering habits should be a part of the solution. I worked at raising my introverted voice in a crowd. I shared my point of view in small gatherings and then branched out to speak up in larger gatherings. Little habits eventually became big habits. Little by little I learned how to be heard and seen and let go of my fear of disagreement. **Voicing my perspective to others helped me practice visibility on a smaller scale.** It helped me get more comfortable taking up space with my views. It helped me work through the many fears I had about what that would mean. Most importantly, it helped me learn how to lead from my perspective in small increments. That was not an easy thing for a shy woman.

*Small Ways to Practice Visibility*
*and Exercise Your Authority*

- The next time you are in a group, speak up and make sure your voice is heard. Be deliberate about sharing your view on issues, especially those that matter to you.
- If you are cut off by somebody in a conversation, quickly remind them that you were speaking and then complete your thought. By doing this, you are conveying a message: What you have to say is important.
- Share your view even if it makes you uncomfortable. Accept that others may disagree with your point of view, but your point of view is still valid.
- Don't be afraid of conflict. There will be times when you are sharing your perspective when others will not agree with you. Remind yourself that conflict is not an indication you've done something wrong, but rather that your view is an important part of the equation and needs to be included in the conversation.
- Say yes to opportunities that allow you to lead and influence others.
- If you read an online article or another piece of public writing you disagree with, respond to the

author of the article, and share your point of view.

- If you find yourself in the middle of an uncomfortable conversation where sexism, racism, or other bigotry is being tolerated, stand up against these things and state your opinion on the matter.
- Look for opportunities to get involved in your community.
- Suggest a solution during a board meeting, say yes to a challenging task, or initiate a conversation with someone who intimidates you.

Each of these actions can help you get out of your comfort zone and strengthen your resolve to be seen as a leader. These habits will lay the foundation for even bigger habits. Building these habits is a lot like body-building—the more you exercise muscles, the stronger they will become. Start by building smaller habits first and then notice how slowly it gets easier to flex bigger habits. Get into the habit of putting yourself and your views in front of others in small ways. This will help you exercise your authority and develop your role as a leader on a larger scale.

### Promote Your Leadership Ideas
### on a Larger Scale

I have noticed that when my clients begin to develop their leadership and become more comfortable taking up space on a smaller scale, they often want to create bigger opportunities to unleash their ideas. Once a client learns how to take up space in the world, she wants to do it again and again. The same thing happened to me. I didn't realize it at the time, but when I said yes to leading the Cru team, I began learning how to take up space in the world. And I've never stopped learning. You can do it, too. Start with small actions and then create bigger opportunities to take up space—to lead and exercise your authority.

When you're ready, look for ways to take up space on a bigger scale. If you're a writer who has kept her content private, publish your material or submit it to a public platform. If you have a yoga license but don't teach classes, find a studio where you can practice leading others through yoga. Start a forum on an issue of social justice that is important to you and change the current political climate. Launch your own TV series; start a clothing line; start a podcast about an issue that is important to you. Pitch your ideas to your boss. Start your own company. Be the boss. Write, dance, run for political office…there are so many ways to be a leader and exercise your authority on a larger scale. How can you use your unique perspective to have a bigger impact on the world and inspire others?

*Platforms: Taking Up Space*
*on a Grander Scale*

To determine how to take up space on a grander scale, you must first decide what you are passionate about. Start by asking yourself, "If I could stand on a stage and deliver a message others could hear, what would I say?" When you have a message that you really want others to hear, build a platform, stand on top of it, and deliver your message with authority. **A platform is a medium that enables you to be seen or heard**. Building a platform is a great way to take up space on a grander scale and reach a larger audience. In today's world, a digital platform that uses a combination of online tools such as a website, social media, and a newsletter, is the most effective way to reach a larger audience with your message. Anyone can create a digital platform, and platforms have helped level the playing field across gender and social status. Writing, publishing, and public speaking are also powerful mediums for amplifying your ideas and thought leadership.

Think back to the moment when you first decided to read this book. What was going on in your life that made you reach for this book instead of all the others competing for your attention? Perhaps the word "empowered" attracted you—because you know you have something important to say and want to be empowered to do it. One way to do so is to build a platform in order to amplify your message and mission.

The most influential leaders attach a higher mission to their goals and ambitions. They aren't in it for self-gain. Here's what I mean by that. Shortly after a gunman opened fire at Stoneman Douglas High School in 2018, killing seventeen of her peers, eighteen-year-old Stoneman Douglas student Emma Gonzales created a platform in order to draw attention to the need for gun control.[3] Her awful experience made her passionate about preventing future school shootings. Emma Gonzales created her Twitter account @Emma4Change four days after the shooting. As she struggled with the emotional aftermath and trauma, she documented her thoughts and experiences on Twitter. With bold vulnerability, she shared what it was like to sit in a classroom for six minutes and twenty seconds as the murderer carried out the shooting spree. She used Twitter to speak publicly to hundreds of thousands of readers, challenging politicians to create legislation on gun control. Soon, Emma had over a million followers on Twitter. She took up space on a grander scale using a digital platform to amplify her mission and voice. She became a leader in the space of gun control advocacy even though she was only a teenager.

Marley Dias, who at age eleven founded the #1000BlackGirlBooks project, was frustrated with the lack of books with black girls as main characters.[4] She had a simple mission. She wanted to collect and donate 1000 books that featured black girls as the main character. Dias used Twitter, Facebook, and a dedicated website to engage others in the task. Dias eventually collected and donated over 12,000 books. As her online presence grew, she received attention from Hillary Clinton, Oprah, Michelle Obama, and Ellen DeGeneres, and she also published her own book, *Marley Dias Gets It Done: And So Can You!* Eleven-year-old Dias started with a simple mission and created a digital platform where she could be seen and heard. She became a leader in the space of representation in publishing.

These women, and many others, accomplished their missions because they were able to build platforms where they could be heard and seen on a grander scale. **All of these women were fueled by their missions**. **They also had**

**something else in common—they were driven less by ego and more by the desire to accomplish something that mattered to them.** The best leaders are often fueled by a purpose and are energized by their passion.

Claiming your authority by building a larger platform requires a lot of energy, commitment, and vulnerability. It often means dealing with pushback, criticism, and self-doubt as well as working through fears around embracing visibility. I understand how it feels to want to make a difference in the world and how hard it can be to navigate those feelings, so I have provided many tools and insights in this book that will help you step into the world on a grander scale and amplify your ideas.

It's important to have clarity on *why* you want to build a platform on a grander scale. Get clear on the message you want to deliver and the reason you want to deliver it. One way to create this clarity is to craft a vision statement. **A vision statement is a descriptive statement that reflects why you want to pursue a specific goal.** It will also help you sustain energy along the way and remind you why taking up space on a grander scale is worth it. I provide a detailed description of how to create a vision statement in Chapter 2, "The Habit of Taking More Risks: How to Get Out of Your Comfort Zone and Overcome Fear."

Although building a platform may sound intimidating, there are many great resources that can help you.[5] You don't have to have a marketing degree to create space for yourself in the world. You just need a lot of grit and determination.

The scale of your platform is not as important as bringing your voice into the world. You don't have to be Oprah or

Emma Gonzales to make a difference. You just need to be you and trust that what you have to say matters. Walk into a room with the full confidence of a woman who believes she belongs there. Speak up with full authority. Build a platform—large or small.

Don't keep yourself hidden; instead, take up space in the world. Use the tools in this book to work through any self-doubt that is keeping you from stepping into leadership: take control of what your body language is communicating to others, store up messages about the importance of women in leadership, and practice visibility by promoting your ideas and putting yourself in situations where you can lead with authority in both big and small ways. Every time you do, you are clearing the way for the next generation of women to be seen and heard. It's time for you to claim your inherent power to lead.

## CHAPTER 6 IN A NUTSHELL

1. The habit of taking up space is a pattern of using your perspective, body language, and voice to claim a position of leadership and authority.

2. Women often experience fear around owning their power, authority, and influence. Some of this tension is born out of the messages they've been taught about what it means to be female and feminine, and how one cannot be feminine and

powerful at the same time. We can change these false messages.

3. When you take up space, you are claiming your inherent power to be a leader.

4. The first element of taking up space is owning your unique perspective on the world. This starts with believing in yourself and knowing who you are. If you don't know yourself and believe in yourself, others will pick up on it. When you walk into a room, you bring all of the beliefs you have about yourself with you.

5. The second element of taking up space is learning how to face any fear about what it means to step into leadership. When you're growing into a person who is owning their authority, fear is a normal part of the process. Some common fears are: What if I sound stupid? What if someone challenges my ideas or what I have to say? or What if I fail? These fears are rooted in the discomfort of being seen and heard.

6. The third element of taking up space is knowing how to use body language to convey that every space you are in is a space you belong in. When you walk into a room your body language can radiate confidence and presence, or it can exude insecurity. Your body tells others how to relate to you before they ever hear your voice. You have the power to exude confidence by taking control of what your body language is communicating to others. When you're getting ready to lead

or to share your perspective, do a body check and make sure you're exuding confidence and authority.

7. The fourth element of taking up space is actively finding ways to promote your leadership style, ideas, and perspective. I call this "practicing visibility." The best way to practice visibility is to start with small actionable steps. I call these "little habits." Remember that what you practice grows stronger. Look for opportunities to practice visibility on a smaller scale. If you do this, over time you will become more comfortable with visibility on a larger scale.

8. A platform is a medium that enables you to be seen or heard on a grander scale. If you have a message that you really want others to hear, build a platform, stand on top of it, and deliver your message with authority. In today's world, a digital platform that uses a combination of online tools such as a website, social media, and a newsletter, is the most effective way to reach a larger audience with your message. Anyone can create a digital platform, and platforms have helped level the playing field across gender and social status.

## QUESTIONS FOR GROUP OR SELF-REFLECTION

1. What is one way you can practice taking up space this week?
2. Tell a story about a moment when you promoted your ideas and perspective.

3. What fear is keeping you from taking another step towards leadership?
4. What does your body behavior reveal about how you feel in this moment?
5. What is the message or mission you want to amplify?
6. If you could stand on a stage and deliver a message others could hear, what would you say?

# CHAPTER 7

# THE HABIT OF KNOWING WHO YOU ARE
## HOW TO CULTIVATE AUTHENTICITY AND SELF-ACCEPTANCE

The first time I watched flamenco, it took hold of me for life. Since then, I've had the obsessive devotion of a zealot and have spent hours observing how flamenco dancers attack space with their bodies and spirit. As part of this obsession, I have been taking flamenco lessons for over a decade, even though I have little natural talent as a dancer. My love for the dance is just that strong.

A few summers ago, I enrolled in a new dance class so I could learn the "soleá" style of flamenco. Its name comes from the word soledad which means loneliness. The soleá rhythm is heavy and slow and mirrors the seriousness of the dancer as she conveys deep emotion and passion. Soleá is typically performed solo, so the artist has more opportunity to show off her individual style of flamenco. It had been a while since I'd danced flamenco, and I was looking forward to embodying the passion, strength, and power that comes from it. It was a sunny summer Chicago day, and we were in a studio with tall windows overlooking the Mexican neighborhood of Pilsen Village. On the first day of class, the head instructor, Wendy Clinard, introduced us to Maria, a flamenco dancer visiting from Spain who would be teaching us the essence of soleá.

As I gazed at Maria, I immediately found myself drawn to her. This weathered Spaniard was captivating and mesmerizing. There was nothing remarkable about her appearance. She was a petite, slightly overweight older woman whose skin revealed a life of struggles. Yet, despite her lack of conventional beauty, she exuded a powerful, magnetic presence.

First, Maria demonstrated the elements of the choreography. Soon after, the air was filled with sound as the metal plates attached to our flamenco shoes hit the wooden dance floor and created the percussive patterns of the compás —that is, the rhythmic musical pattern specific to soleá. I felt my muscles waking up, my body coming out of a long hibernation as it breathed in the powerful force of flamenco. Fifteen minutes later Maria broke my trance when she stopped class and asked us all to take a seat on the floor. I was irritated by the interruption, but, dutifully, I sat. She said:

> In order to dance soleá, you must first understand the
> heart of the dance. You can learn all the dance steps,
> work with the best guitarist, master the choreography,
> master the percussive elements of the feet, and wear a
> breathtaking dress. However, in order to truly express
> the soleá style, you must also embody who you are as
> a person. You must know who you are and express
> your inner self throughout the dance. Only then can

you convey the essence of soleá. Otherwise, they are merely dance steps.

Once Maria began to speak, I was drawn to the wisdom of her spirit and the power of her words, which will forever be emblazoned in my mind. I didn't realize then that what she said would change me forever.

You see, soleá is the expression of your soul with wild abandon through dance. If you want to dance soleá you must reveal your presence to the audience as if saying, "I am here, visible, my soul in plain sight." You need to own who you are at the core and reveal it within the expression of the movement. In fact, the best soleá dancers know how to enter the space of their audience, command the room with their presence, and own the stage because they know who they are and express it through the movement of their body. So, if you want to dance soleá style, you must have duende — you must know who you are and be able to confidently express it to others.

Listening to her, I experienced a holy moment. The room was still, and I was drawn into a deep pool of self-reflection. I asked myself: "Do I truly know who I am? Can I confidently express the essence of who I am not just on the dance floor, but more importantly, on the dance floor called life?"

As Oprah would say, listening to Maria's speech was an *a-ha* moment. You see, we're all on the dance floor of life. And how we show up on the dance floor really matters. We can be meek and hide behind our insecurities. We can passively mimic a well-learned choreography. Or we can confidently and powerfully express who we are through our movements, interactions, and voice. Maria's lesson about how to embrace the essence of soleá by embracing who we are was also a lesson about how to live life authentically.

After I listened to my dance instructor's words, I was eager to express the essence of soleá—both as a flamenco dancer and in my personal life. I spent that entire summer focused on the habit of cultivating a deeper knowledge of who I was and becoming more comfortable in my own skin. In the end, I never did perfect the compás, which is the rhythmic structure of the flamenco footwork. I struggled with mastering the intricate hand, arm, and body movements. However, I wasn't worried. Maria taught me that learning the intricacies of flamenco wasn't the point. So, at the end of summer, on the day of our student performance, I wasn't nervous. I stepped onto the dance floor and commanded the room with my presence. I executed the dance without apology, fully owning my imperfect movements. I held the gaze of my audience as if I were shouting, "I am here! Do you see me?" I fully expressed the essence of who I was as I danced flamenco with wild abandon for the first time in my life. I had duende! I began to understand who I was and learned how to express myself with commanding confidence.

In this chapter, I show you how to cultivate a deeper knowledge of who you are. Self-knowledge leads to self-acceptance and duende—a Spanish word used in flamenco dancing to refer to an authentic, passionate, and confident expression of yourself. There are four habits that cultivate that kind of bold inner attitude.

The first habit is living authentically. Authenticity means being your true self and making sure your insides match your outside. It can be tempting to be someone you're not when doing so leads to affirmation. However, nothing is more important or powerful that just being you.

The second habit is embracing imperfections. Perfectionist thinking leads to massive self-judgement. None of us are perfect, and we all have things about ourselves we tend to dislike. However, in order to truly embrace who we are, we need to accept all of who we are, including the messy and scruffy parts.

The third habit is investing in self-awareness. Self-awareness sets the foundation for living authentically and is key to understanding who you are at the core. I will share several of my favorite tools that cost very little but yield lots of valuable personalized insights.

The fourth habit is using self-talk for self-compassion and self-acceptance. The way we talk to ourselves has a big impact on how we think about ourselves. When it comes to self-talk, we can be our own friend and foe. Our internal dialogue can bolster self-confidence and sabotage it. Learning how to engage in compassionate self-talk can make a big difference in feeling good about ourselves.

Additionally, I will share specific suggestions regarding how to hold on tight to your identity if you happen to be a woman who is in the season of active parenting. Collectively, these habits and insights will empower you to show up on the dance floor fully knowing and confidently expressing who you are.

## DUENDE: A CONFIDENT EXPRESSION OF WHO YOU ARE

I can attest to the magic that happens when a flamenco dancer is in full possession of the room, commanding the attention of the audience with each stomp of her feet and sway of her arm. The magic doesn't come from dancing with perfection, but from a willingness to dance with wild abandon and in full possession of who she is, radiating confidence and a bold attitude.

As I mentioned earlier, in flamenco, we say this kind of dancer has "duende." **Duende is a Spanish word used in flamenco dancing to refer to an authentic, passionate, and confident expression of who you are**. It requires bravely showing up as your authentic self, allowing yourself to be seen, and being vulnerable all at the same time.

You might not be a flamenco dancer, but you can still have duende. You, too, can be authentic and confident, so much so that it inspires others and draws them toward you. Duende comes from having two qualities: knowing who you are and expressing who you are with confidence. In addition to having duende, there are many benefits that come from having a deep-seated knowledge of who you are at the core.

*The Benefits of Knowing Who You Are*

- Knowing who you are increases acceptance of

oneself without qualifications, exceptions, or conditions.

- Knowing who you are reduces self-criticism and the type of self-injurious thinking that can wreak havoc on one's identity. This type of thinking leads you to believe you're not good enough, capable enough, smart enough, and so on.
- The more you understand the nuances of your personality, the easier it is to appreciate characteristics you might otherwise vilify.
- When you know who you are it is easier to execute other powerful habits, such as expressing your viewpoint with confidence, making decisions that are aligned with your values, setting boundaries, being vulnerable, and being assertive.

The most common characteristic of successful people is self-awareness.[1] One of the best investments you can make is to take the time to know thyself.

## AUTHENTICITY MEANS BEING YOUR TRUE SELF

One day, I asked my sage friend Susan what being authentic meant to her.

She said, "I try to make sure my insides match my outsides."

Hers was the best definition of authenticity I had ever heard. **Authenticity means being your true self and making**

**sure who you are on the inside matches who you are on the outside**.

Never hide your authentic self in order to be likable. Women in particular often do this to themselves. At times, it can be tempting to be someone we're not because, in the moment, it feels good to be liked. It's normal to desire the approval of others; however, make sure doing so doesn't keep you from being your authentic self. Being considered likable by others is not worth more than liking yourself. Instead of investing in being popular, invest in knowing who you are. In the long run, it's so much more empowering.

Here's one way to think about what it means to invest in being yourself instead of being likable. Chameleons are reptiles that change the color of their skin in order to blend into their environment, making it difficult to see them. Ask yourself: have you ever been like a chameleon—blending instead of showing your true colors, remaining silent instead of speaking up when you disagreed with others, pretending to have it all together instead of admitting you were struggling and needing help? Most of us have had moments when we chose to blend in and hide our true selves, just like a chameleon. When we do this, we are placing more value on seeking approval instead of being genuine.

There are many ways we might engage in chameleon-like tendencies. We might blend into our existing environment by conforming to the culture we live in. We might alter our values, fashion, theology, beliefs about gender, or political preferences in order to fit in. We do this because blending in or hiding parts of who we are can sometimes feel more comfortable than revealing our authentic selves. The problem with blending in is, just like the chameleon, we can become invisible, indistinguishable from others around us, and, most importantly, ignore our true selves. It's far better to stand out and reveal your own true colors.

I grew up in New Mexico belonging to a unique Latin and indigenous sub-culture, known for being artistic, flamboyant, and creative. My people wear cotton clothing stitched with extravagantly decorative embroidery, vibrantly colored boots, weathered jeans, big belts, big hats, and layers upon layers of turquoise and silver jewelry. I was twenty-two years old when I moved to the Midwest in the late 1980s in order to attend graduate school in the suburb of Wheaton, Illinois. At that time, Wheaton's population was ninety-nine percent white. I was part of a community of non-white people that comprised less than one percent of the population.

I arrived in the suburbs with a suitcase full of bohemian blouses, embroidered tops, and leather-trimmed hats, and another suitcase filled with the silver and turquoise jewelry I had carefully collected. I soon discovered I would be living in the land of nautical stripes, penny loafers, polo shirts, and pastel cardigans. The culture of the Midwest suburbs was vastly different from the predominantly indigenous and predominantly poor farming community I grew up in. For the first time in my life, I felt like I didn't fit in. Not just because of my flamboyant bohemian clothing, but because of the brown color of my skin.

I remember shopping in a local clothing store in downtown Wheaton, and the store associate asked me if I was taking on more clients. As the conversation continued, I realized this woman had assumed I was a local cleaning lady.

It never occurred to this store clerk that a young brown woman was a local student pursuing a master's degree in clinical psychology.

From the minute I arrived at Wheaton College, I was acutely aware I was very different from my mostly white, mostly wealthy, mostly suburban peers. I was poor, brown, and rural. I was twenty-two years old, unsure of myself, and still discovering who I was. At some point, I decided that fitting in felt better than standing out. My inner chameleon took over and I began to wear pastel cardigans, capris, and penny loafers instead of my normal clothing. My desire to fit in, and my desire for the approval of others, trumped my willingness to be authentic.

Looking back, I wonder if I thought wearing clothing that I associated with "being white" made me think my brown skin would blend in more. Friends, it didn't. Instead, I just looked awkward, as if I was wearing somebody else's clothing rather than my own. I had dimmed the light on my true identity. I was like a chameleon—blending in instead of showing my true colors. I was not a white Midwestern preppy woman. My true self was a wild-hearted-bohemian-brown-skinned-woman who loved colorful, bold clothing. My problem was not that I was wearing the wrong clothing, but rather that I was not wearing my true identity.

My cultural identity and brown skin did stand out in a very white world—but that was okay. My Latina inheritance raced through every fiber of my being. It influenced my values; it was the undercurrent of many of my struggles. My heritage made me, well—me! I was different from the suburban, proper, conservative Midwesterners who dominated Wheaton. Eventually, I embraced my identity and shed the cardigans, returning to wearing big hats and colorful clothing buried beneath layers of turquoise, the state gemstone of New Mexico.

Have you ever set aside the real you in order to fit in? It feels good for a while, but eventually the feeling of not-being-good-enough-just-as-you-are settles in. It's better to just be your authentic self. Instead of blending in like a chameleon, boldly express who you are. **Instead of doing things you hope will make you more likable, take the time to understand your personality and embrace your true identity.** Blending in to feel likable is a short-sighted goal. The most likable people are those who possess self-acceptance, authenticity and duende!

Obviously, authenticity means a whole lot more than simply making sure your clothing expresses your personality. Authenticity means being your true self and making sure your insides match your outside. It's about owning your perspective, embracing your cultural identity, defining your values, politics, theology, and beliefs overall. Embracing your identity and being authentic will help you feel confident and be confident. It will also encourage a genuine connection with others.

Another key ingredient to living authentically includes accepting all of who you are—including the things that are less-than-perfect. Self-acceptance and being authentic work in tandem. So, you're not perfect…so what? Let's talk about a mindset that makes room for your beautiful imperfections.

## SO YOU'RE NOT PERFECT...OH WELL!

The pursuit of perfection is an elusive, unattainable goal. Period. It's like running a marathon that has no finish line. There may be people along the route cheering you on, participating in the false belief that you are actually getting somewhere. You'll be energized by the cheers and accolades you receive from bystanders, but the inevitability of never crossing the finish line awaits you. **There is no end to the race called "the pursuit of perfection." It only leads to the inevitable intersection of self-doubt, self-judgment, and non-acceptance**. It's a tiring, endless, exhausting, and sometimes dangerous race. I don't recommend it. Instead of trying to be perfect, simply accept that you are not and embrace your imperfections.

**Perfectionism is a tendency to set personal standards that are so high they either cannot be met, or only met with great difficulty.** It's a tendency to see even minor imperfections in oneself as not acceptable or horrible. If you've ever felt the need to be perfect, appear perfect, or perform perfectly...you've stumbled upon the trap of perfectionist thinking. If it has become a habit, you've also probably struggled with the lack of self-acceptance that comes from measuring one's self-worth by unreasonable and unattainable standards.

Creating a healthy identity means accepting all of who you are, including the messy and imperfect sides. The first step in letting go of perfectionist thinking is to adjust your standards. Give yourself permission to be good enough. Accept that being imperfect is part of what it means to be human. The good news is there are 7.6 billion other humans in the world who are also imperfect. Welcome to the imperfect-human-club; you fit right in. Instead of setting unreasonable standards on yourself, include your flaws into an acceptable interpretation of what it means to be human.

Another way to let go of perfectionist habits is to think about how your messy and unkempt self can add a beautiful dimension to what makes you unique. For example, I love artwork that expresses the beautiful tension between these two dichotomies: perfection and imperfection. Sun-filled landscapes with sprawling fields of perfectly painted sunflowers make for pleasant artwork. However, I am more inspired by artwork I call "ugly-beautiful" because this style of artwork reflects how these dichotomies can create more powerful and inspiring images. Frida Kahlo's edgy artwork is a good example of ugly-beautiful art. Her paintings often include images of golden desert landscapes, bold Mexican flowers, exotic animals; but these beautiful things are portrayed alongside vivid images of skulls, death, pain, blood, and suffering. Frida's artwork often reflects the tension between two polarities—things we love and things we hate. Yet somehow, she creates harmony between things that are ugly and beautiful. **This type of artwork reveals how imperfection can live in harmony with beauty to create something even more beautiful.** That is why I love ugly-beautiful artwork—it reflects how the things we love about ourselves, our struggles and weaknesses, and our perfections and imperfections, can live in harmony.

Think about yourself as a beautiful piece of artwork. You are human artwork. You are a spectacular blend of beautiful, messy, edgy, brilliant, colorful images—all coming together to create a marvelous masterpiece that is perfectly ugly-beautiful.

Blend the unattractive and attractive parts of who you are, your strengths and weaknesses, and all the good, messy, flawed, and brilliant sides of who you are at this moment into an original piece of living artwork that others are drawn to. Need inspiration? Think about Malala Yousafzai, who, as a young girl living in Pakistan, was shot in the face by the Taliban because she was an activist for women's education in an environment that did not value women.[2] She incorporated her scars, her history, her personality, and her passion into a movement. She gave meaning and purpose to a tragic experience. Every woman has some Malala inside of her, but she first needs to own and integrate all of who she is: her story, personality, quirks, passions, and pain. Human artwork is inspiring.

So, you're not perfect, so what? Embrace all your strengths, weaknesses, imperfections, and vulnerabilities as part of your multidimensional strength and beauty. Own those murky and gray parts of who you are—not just the shiny and sparkly sides.

*A Coaching Moment:*
*An Expressive Art Activity*

This expressive art activity is a fun way to imagine including all aspects of who you are through art. Before you start this activity, ask your inner critic to leave the room—there is no room for her here. This exercise is all about having fun and seeing what happens when you engage in some low-key expressive art. Before you get started make sure you have a pen, a few sheets of blank paper and either crayons or markers handy.

1. Write down a list of the things you like about yourself.

2. Next, create another list of the things about yourself that you are struggling to accept.

3. Next, using crayons or markers, create an image of yourself that includes things from both of your lists—the things you like about yourself and the things you are struggling to accept. The goal is to draw an inspiring image of yourself that blends all of who you are—the messy, the imperfect, the vulnerable, and the strong. Draw your image on a blank sheet of paper.

4. Finally, take a minute to reflect on your self-portrait of "human art." What inspires you about your drawing? How does this self-portrait help you take one step towards self-acceptance?

Embracing all of who you are is an attainable goal with a finish line. It doesn't mean you should stop trying to be the best person you can be. It means the way you evaluate yourself is not dependent on the goals you set for yourself. You are already acceptable just the way you are in this moment.

## EMPOWERED WOMEN INVEST IN SELF-AWARENESS

Can you imagine looking in a mirror and not seeing your own reflection? Until you really know who you are, you are living your life without seeing an accurate image of your inner self. **Self-awareness is having an accurate and honest understanding of who you are**. It includes being aware of your traits, values, and feelings. It also includes understanding how you make decisions, how you take in information, your personal triggers, where you get your energy, what makes you want to do the happy dance, and more.

Once you know who you are on the inside, you will feel more comfortable in your skin. You will be more self-accepting and less prone to falling into the bitter trap of perfectionism. When you know who you are, you will be able to learn what you need to thrive; therefore, you will be less likely to engage in unhealthy patterns, such as people-pleasing. Self-awareness leads to clarity on your unique perspective, thoughts, and ideas, thus giving you more ownership of them. Self-awareness is the key that unlocks the door to radiant self-confidence. These are just a few of the many benefits that come from knowing who you are. That's why empowered women practice the habit of self-awareness.

There are many ways to increase self-awareness. I have noticed many of my clients have a natural ability to be introspective and self-examining. However, when it comes to self-awareness, candid objectivity is necessary. Objectivity can help us see things we might otherwise have difficulty seeing.

We all have blind spots. We all can benefit from an impartial perspective in our understanding of how we function, how others perceive us, our strengths and weaknesses, and other key aspects of self-awareness. There are many great resources for developing this habit; the following is a list of my six favorites. I love these tools because they are affordable, easily accessible, and focus more on strengths instead of weaknesses. These tools can deliver tons of insights for a small investment. I have used all of these tools with my coaching clients. I recommend tapping into at least one tool every year. Regular self-awareness check-ups will provide a steady stream of insights into who you are.

**Myers-Briggs Inventory**

My absolute favorite tool for increasing self-awareness is the Myers-Briggs Inventory (myersbriggs.org). When I became a certified Myers-Briggs practitioner several years ago, I was floored by the magnitude of insights the resource provides. The Myers-Briggs Inventory is a self-report questionnaire designed to help you determine which of the sixteen personality types best describes how you function. The assessment focuses on eight personality preferences, grouped in pairs: introvert and extrovert, sensing and intuition, thinking and feeling, and judging and perceiving. These preferences are psychological functions that have a lot to do with how people perceive and operate in the world.

This personality inventory is exceptionally effective at establishing acceptance of your idiosyncratic behaviors that can be easily misunderstood or villainized. It will help you understand where you get your energy, how you make decisions, and which environments can bring out the best in you. It describes the process you use for taking in new information. It reveals why some situations may leave you feeling tongue-tied and temporarily out-of-sync. You will discover what boosts your energy and what depletes it. The Myers-Briggs Inventory can boost both your self-awareness and self-acceptance.

After you discover your Myer-Briggs type, learn about it. You can subscribe to a newsletter based on your four-letter type; a simple Google search will help you do this. YouTube has lots of five-minute descriptions of each of the sixteen personality types, which can enhance your knowledge of your specific type.

### Emotional Intelligence 2.0

*Emotional Intelligence 2.0*, by Travis Bradberry and Jean Greaves, is a fabulous book that provides a roadmap for understanding and developing emotional intelligence ("E.Q."). Emotional Intelligence is an accumulation of four attributes: self-awareness, social awareness, self-management, and social management. This book goes beyond simply describing what E.Q. is and why it matters. It includes an online assessment that can be accessed with a unique code in the back of each book. This code allows the reader to log onto a website and upload a personalized emotional intelligence assessment. The assessment measures how the reader ranks in each of the four emotional intelligence measures. This extra tool provides the reader the opportunity to increase their own

E.Q. as they work through each exercise provided in the book. Understanding the value of emotional intelligence and how it is related to how you view yourself and how others view you is a powerful way to enhance self-awareness.

### Strength Finders

*Strength Finders,* a popular book by Tom Rath and Don Clifton, is a valuable tool for discovering your natural gifts and propensities. This book is not a simple touchy-feely-feel-good read. Instead, it is the accumulation of decades of research by Don Clifton, who studied and categorized the gifts of the most successful people in the world. This book describes, with great detail, each of the thirty-four strengths he discovered. The strengths are organized into four categories—strategic thinking, relationship building, influencing, and executing. The book details how a person's individual strengths function in each of these categories and then describes how our own strengths can best be enhanced. Examples of some of the personality strengths described in this book are analytical, harmonizing, achieving, and maximizing. This book includes a coupon code that can be used to take an online assessment that details the reader's top five strengths. It's a powerful book that can expose hidden strengths, improve confidence, and build on personal awareness.

### Spiritual Gifts Inventory

If you are a person of faith, you may want to know your

spiritual gifts. Spiritual gifts are unique strengths that can enhance the spiritual growth of others and are commonly acknowledged and utilized within the Christian tradition. Some examples of spiritual gifts are teaching, spiritual direction, healing, hospitality, and prayer. Rock Church in San Diego offers a free online spiritual gifts assessment that I recommend (giftstest.com). The assessment was designed by their pastoral team with the goal of helping others understand their spiritual gifts as well as how to apply these gifts to their community. If you are a part of this spiritual community, it can be helpful to expand your awareness of your unique spiritual gifts.

**Creative Endeavors**

Engaging in creative activities can lead to extraordinary self-discovery. When I decided to learn how to dance flamenco, my intention was very simple—I wanted to immerse myself in an art form I had been obsessed with for years. What I soon learned, however, is that when we engage in any artistic or creative endeavor, we are also engaging in a process of self-discovery. In my practice, I have heard many similar stories from my clients.

One of my clients realized that the ridged lines in her artwork often mimicked the rigidity of her own unbending rules and principles. Another client, who was an equestrian rider, discovered that her horse was very sensitive to her emotional life, often imitating her mood with a sigh, neigh, or a skittish gallop. This helped her realize the effect her moods could have on others.

Flamenco helped me learn the importance of self-awareness, and how that knowledge is expressed through dance movement. I frequently left dance class fortified with new insights related to my identity. In my TEDx talk, "How to Quiet a Shame-Producing Toxic Voice," I shared several of these insights—and I also danced a little flamenco in order to demonstrate how dancing helped me realize the amount of shame I was living with (bit.ly/margotedx).

Creative endeavors include many activities: yoga, singing, expressive dance, songwriting, writing, art, improv comedy, horseback riding, and pottery. These are just a few examples. Creative endeavors enhance self-awareness in a number of ways. These kinds of activities stimulate the brain regions responsible for connecting feelings, imagination, problem-solving, and holistic thinking, often resulting in powerful insights. Creative experiences also nurture the relationship you have with yourself, arguably the most important relationship in your life. Creativity can cause us to examine what inspires us and motivates us. Self-awareness is one of the many benefits that can emerge from quieting the logical mind and activating the creative mind.

### Enneagram

The Enneagram (eneagraminstitute.com) is a personality inventory that reveals patterns of how people interpret the world. It can help increase your knowledge of your core motivations. It describes a set of nine distinct personality types, with a number denoting each type. It offers useful insights into motivations and relationship patterns, and how different Enneagram types relate to one another. Once you discover your Enneagram number, there are many online forums and blogs that expand on each personality type. Many businesses and churches use the Enneagram to enhance team-building and to create appreciation for fellow team members.

### Counseling and Coaching

Many of my clients come into my office wanting to resolve a variety of issues such as anxiety, relational issues, or job dissatisfaction. They soon discover there is a connection between resolving their presenting problem and being self-aware. As their self-awareness grows, the resolution to their problem often emerges. The more they learn about who they are, the more empowered they feel to resolve what concerns them. They also notice that their self-knowledge and self-confidence often grow in tandem. **Self-awareness generates all kinds of power**.

Coaching and counseling are two powerful tools for increasing self-awareness and self-acceptance. If you don't have the resources to afford individual counseling, let your trusted inner circle know you are looking for a coach or counselor who would be willing to see you on a sliding scale. Coaches and counselors almost always set aside a portion of their time to provide their services pro-bono or at a reduced fee. A dash of tenacity can lead to finding a seasoned coach or counselor who can guide you toward personal insights and powerful self-discovery.

As I have shown here, there are numerous tools available

that can help you understand who you are. Get into the habit of investing in self-awareness. **The habit of knowing who you are will give rise to embracing your true self.** It will empower you to embody duende—the ability to express who you are with powerful confidence. Be intentional and commit to objective input and an investment of time and resources. The investment will yield incredible benefits and embolden you to own the power that comes with being you.

## SELF-TALK HAS A LOT TO DO WITH THE RELATIONSHIP YOU HAVE WITH YOURSELF

We've all heard the maxim that the way we talk to others will determine the relationship we have with them. Did you know the way you talk to yourself will also influence the relationship you have with yourself? Because the longest and most important relationship you will ever have will be with yourself, learning how to engage in encouraging and compassionate self-talk is essential.

**The way we talk to ourselves has a lot to do with how we think about ourselves.** If your self-talk is full of self-compassion and kindness, you are more likely to feel more confident and self-accepting. If your inner critic dominates your self-talk, most likely your self-esteem gets regular beatings. **Self-criticism produces shame, and shame can destroy the human heart.**

Most of us have an inner critic looming within us that needs to be tamed and replaced with a kinder, gentler inner voice. When we show ourselves compassion and kindness, we begin to change the way we see ourselves. Self-acceptance and self-talk work in tandem.

An inner critic can wreak havoc on your confidence and self-acceptance. I refer to the inner critic as "Ms. Critical." Have you met her? Perhaps you are even good friends with her.

**This is what Ms. Critical's voice sounds like:**

- "You are making a fool of yourself."
- "You are not smart enough to do that!"
- "Everybody is skinnier than you."
- "You're not good enough."
- "That was stupid."
- "Why did you do that?"
- "You should have…"
- "You'll never…"
- "You don't belong."

Do you recognize the voice of Ms. Critical? That's what she might sound like inside of your head. The truth is, you would probably *never* talk to someone else as harshly as you talk to yourself. Yet we talk to ourselves with the voice of criticism all the time. Ms. Critical is a powerful bully that chips away at self-confidence and self-acceptance.

The only voice to whom Ms. Critical will yield is the voice of compassion. I refer to this inner voice as "Ms. Compassion." Ms. Compassion is the voice inside of you that is more caring, kind, and gracious.

**This is what Ms. Compassion's voice sounds like:**

- "It's okay, everybody makes mistakes."
- "Be kind to yourself, you did your best."
- "I am here for you and I'm going to take care of you."
- "Your heart was in the right place when you made that decision."
- "I'm so proud of you."
- "It's going to be okay."
- "You don't have to be perfect."

You have probably said similar words of encouragement to the people in your life whom you care about. But—do you ever talk to yourself like this? If so, you've probably noticed that being self-compassionate has a powerful effect on keeping Ms. Critical at bay. Engaging in the type of self-talk that is gracious, compassionate, and clothed in self-acceptance can have a big impact on how we feel about ourselves.

*A Coaching Moment:*
*The Power of Self-Compassion*

This surprisingly simple, but very powerful practice I'm about to share with you can help you become more aware of your self-talk and demonstrate how to engage in a specific type of self-talk that encourages self-compassion. This mindfulness exercise can help quiet your inner critic. Try it for thirty days and notice how it changes the way you think about yourself.

1. The first step is to become more aware of the moments you're being hard on yourself and then to notice what your inner critic sounds like. For example, your inner critic might sound like "You should have…" or "What's wrong with you?" or "I can't believe you did that."

2. Second, when you notice your inner critic is active and making you feel bad about yourself, try talking to yourself with more kindness. Compassionate self-talk should include words bathed in patience and grace. For example, this inner self-talk might sound like, "You are doing your best," "Your heart was in the right place," or "It's okay to make mistakes."

3. If you want to take this practice one step further, add this component. Place your right hand directly over your heart, close your eyes, and take three deep breaths, allowing for a moment of quiet in between each breath. Speaking out loud and to yourself, recall your voice of compassion and invite it to respond to the inner critic that is bullying you. For example, you might say to yourself, "You showed a lot of courage." My favorite phrase when I do this is, "Margo, I'm here for you, and it's going to be okay."

Sit quietly for a few minutes and breathe. Let your

words of compassion sink in. With your hand still
placed over your heart and your eyes closed, repeat
the words to yourself a few more times, allowing them
to settle into your heart and mind.

When you engage in this practice, you might feel nothing,
or it might bring tears to your eyes. Just allow the experience
to speak to you in whatever way it does. Practice this habit
for thirty days every time you notice your inner critic is
bullying you. Invite your voice of compassion to speak to you
using this hand-over-heart technique. Over time you will
notice that cultivating self-compassion can have a significant
impact on how you view yourself. In other words, you'll
notice how self-talk can change the relationship you have
with yourself.

## HOLD ONTO YOUR IDENTITY DURING MOTHERHOOD

If you're a stay-at-home mom, I have a specific message for
you regarding how to nurture your identity during the season
of active parenting. Before I share it, it's important to know
that I am a mother who has experienced many phases of
motherhood: being a full-time stay-at-home mom as well as a
mother who worked both part-time and full-time while
raising two kids. I am currently in the "empty nest" season of
parenthood. In other words, I have experienced every
variation of working and not working while actively
parenting. In addition to my own experience, I have
counseled    thousands    of    women    in    every    stage    of

motherhood. It is from this collective experience that I noticed a pattern: **stay-at-home moms who continue to invest in their identity outside the home fare better than those who stop investing in their identity outside the home.** Specifically, women who invest in themselves outside the home tend to have a more confident and self-assured identity. In contrast, I have noticed women who stop investing in their identity outside of their role as a mother are more prone to struggle with self-doubt and report feeling less self-assured.

What I have described may or may not be your experience. However, if this is your experience, consider this advice: if you're struggling with feeling inconsequential, it might have something to do with whether you're investing in your identity outside of your role as a mom. Humans are multi-faceted beings who need to nourish the various aspects of who we are beyond the role of motherhood. During the season of active parenting, make sure to invest in your identity outside your role as a mom. This investment will pay off for yourself and your family.

If you happen to be the kind of woman who would feel guilty for taking family time and resources to invest in yourself, consider this—investing in yourself outside the home will make you a more well-rounded, confident woman and therefore make you a better mother. Everybody benefits when you invest in yourself!

If your confidence level comes primarily from being a mother, then your self-assuredness might be too dependent on the success of your kids. For example, if your son comes home with an A+, you might experience a boost in your confidence. But if he comes home with a note from the teacher stating he doesn't get along with his peers—your self-confidence might vacillate. **It's important to separate your children's behavior from how you measure your self-worth.**

Don't lose yourself during motherhood—down the road, you will need you. Invest time and resources in the things you love that remind you that you are more than a mom. Investing in the things you love to do will also prepare you for the empty nest years when your primary job will not be "mother." Consider this—if you live until the age of 80, you will spend the first quarter of your life not being a parent, then the next quarter of your life actively parenting, and the final *half* of your life inactively parenting (supporting but not being responsible for your adult children). That means seventy percent of your life, the majority, will *not* be spent actively parenting. Don't wait until your empty nest years to invest in your identity outside of your role as a mom.

I have seen very busy moms with limited resources find many ways to invest in their I'm-not-just-a-mom identity.

**Examples of Moms Who Maintained Their Self-Identities:**

- Magdalena volunteered three hours a week at a local horse therapy farm that helped kids with autism.
- Melissa used her innovative design skills to construct a facelift for their school's library, creating imaginative spaces and increasing usage of the library by eighty percent.
- Sue launched a vintage antique shop in a shared

space so that she only had to be in her store a few hours a week. She was able to run the majority of her business from her home.

- Elizabeth volunteered a few hours a week at a nursing home that catered to seniors with Alzheimer's disease and dementia. She did this in memory of her mom who died of Alzheimer's.
- Cecilia became a gourmet cook and used her gifts to entertain friends and inspire her family to spend time together in the kitchen.
- Flavia used her training as a lawyer to advocate for abused women. She also tapped into her circle of friends to raise funds for local women's shelters.
- Charlotte used her skills as a photographer to capture moments between friends and family and timeless memories for her son's swimming team.

There are so many ways to nurture your identity outside of motherhood. Train for a marathon, take an art class, learn Spanish online, teach English as a second language at your local college, teach a bible study at your church, or take a tap-dancing class. Determine today to invest in your identity in addition to your role as a mom. It will be one of the best investments you will ever make.

## CHAPTER 7 IN A NUTSHELL

1. The habit of knowing who you are is a pattern of cultivating self-awareness and authenticity.

2. Duende is a Spanish word used in flamenco dancing to refer to an authentic and confident expression of who you are. You might not be a flamenco dancer, but you can still have duende. Duende comes from having two qualities: knowing who you are and then expressing who you are with contagious confidence.

3. Authenticity means being your true self and making sure who you are on the inside matches who you are on the outside. It's about owning your perspective and embracing your identity. The more you embrace who you are, the more you will possess self-acceptance, confidence, and duende.

4. It's normal to desire the approval of others; however, make sure doing so doesn't keep you from being your authentic self. Being considered likable by others is not worth more than liking yourself. Instead of investing in being likable, invest in knowing who you are and really embracing your true self.

5. Knowing who you are and having self-awareness work in tandem. Self-awareness is having an accurate and honest understanding of who you are. Self-awareness is power. It includes things like being aware of your traits, values, and

feelings, understanding how you make decisions and take information in, knowing your personal triggers, where you get your energy, and what makes you want to do the happy dance.

6. Perfectionist thinking inevitably leads to self-doubt and self-criticism. Perfectionism is a tendency to set personal standards that are so high they either cannot be met, or are met only with great difficulty. It is a tendency to see even minor imperfections in oneself as unacceptable or horrible. If perfectionism has become a habit, you've also probably struggled with the lack of self-acceptance that comes from measuring one's self-worth by unreasonable and unattainable standards. Give yourself permission to be imperfect. It's part of what it means to be human.

7. Creating a healthy identity means accepting all of who you are, including the messy and imperfect parts. The first step in letting go of perfectionist thinking is to adjust your standards. The second step is to understand how your scruffy, unkempt, and imperfect characteristics make you unique. Then incorporate these characteristics into your identity.

8. The way you talk to yourself has a lot to do with how you think about yourself. If your self-talk is bathed in self-compassion and kindness, you are more likely to feel more confident and self-accepting. If your inner critic dominates your self-talk, most likely your self-esteem will be negatively affected by critical self-talk.

9. Stay-at-home moms who continue to invest in their identity outside of their roles as mothers are more likely to feel confident and self-assured. Don't lose yourself during motherhood—down the road, you will need you. Invest time and resources in the things you love—things that remind you that you are more than a mom. Investing in the things you love to do will also prepare you for the empty nest years when your primary job will not be a mother.

## QUESTIONS FOR GROUP OR SELF-REFLECTION

1. Describe a moment when you experienced "duende"—that is, a moment when you fully expressed who you were with powerful confidence.
2. Has self-awareness, or learning about who you are, helped you feel more confident?
3. Do your insides match your outside? If not, what is one step you can take to match your insides with your outside?
4. When, where, or with whom are you most likely to force yourself to blend in instead of being yourself?
5. How do you put pressure on yourself to meet unreasonable standards?
6. If you are a stay-at-home mom, how are you investing in your identity outside of your role as mom?

# CHAPTER 8

# THE HABIT OF LISTENING TO YOUR BODY'S VOICE
## HOW TO LIVE IN TANDEM WITH YOUR BODY

As my son Francisco was preparing to leave for college, I was preparing to arrive in the world of empty nesting. I had decided to face this experience head-on. Part of this plan included returning to activities I never had time for as a working mom. Learning flamenco dancing was at the top of the list. I was giddy with excitement after signing up for my first flamenco class in Chicago. I needed the excitement and longed for the distraction. Since then, I have been a flamenco student for over a decade and have left many flamenco classes with insights that dramatically shaped both my personal and professional life.

One of the classes I signed up for was a technique class designed to teach us the upper body movement of flamenco dancing. Each week we spent sixty minutes engaging in repetitive drills intended to create the muscle memory of the bolero posture. This posture meant dancing with our arms in an open position with our shoulder blades touching and our chests perched high, open, and exposed.

On the first day of the technique class, we ended by sitting on the dance floor to stretch our bodies. Oddly, the minute I sank into child's pose, a yoga movement designed to rest the body in between moves, involuntary tears began to flow down my face. I didn't know what to make of this reaction. My emotional state was fine upon arrival. I brushed it off, quickly wiped my tears, and sheepishly snuck out of class.

The following week, the same thing happened. After sixty minutes of engaging in upper body movement, specifically lifting our chests and extending our arms, the unstoppable tears reappeared at the end of class when I was on the ground resting in child's pose. I remember thinking, "What is wrong with me? What is happening to me?" Once more, I quickly wiped the tears from my eyes and quietly dashed out of class.

Week three was the same scenario…dance drills followed by more tears as I stretched and rested in child's pose. Except by week three I had had enough. I decided to figure out what was happening to me. This time I waited until all my classmates left the studio and sought out the wisdom of my dance instructor, Wendy Clinard.

After I told her about my emotional reaction, she shared something I will never forget. "In order to dance flamenco, you will need to be able to open up your body, chest, and arms. When you invite your body to do this, you are engaging in physical vulnerability. If you're finding it difficult to stay in the 'open position,' that is, chest forward and upright with arms opened wide, it is because your body is resisting the experience of vulnerability. Your body is speaking to you. Your tears are the body's reaction to the vulnerability of being open and exposed. Your body wants to stay closed because it has emotional pain. Is there something personal you need to work through that you have been resisting or avoiding?"

Oh boy…next came the ugly cry—a heavy and unstoppable unattractive barrel of tears. My resistance quickly faded. I knew the feelings I had been avoiding. I was dreading the departure of my son Francisco and the loss of his presence. I had noticed Francisco pulling away from me and shutting me out. I was afraid we would lose our close relationship when he left for college. Instead of giving myself permission to grieve I had been letting my inner tough girl take charge. Suddenly my inner sad-mom-missing-her-son was out in the open and in charge. And she was crying in dance class. It was the beginning of learning how to listen to my body's voice and how to use it to pay attention to what I was feeling and needing.

**Our bodies will never lie. They will always tell us what we feel and need…if we listen.** Our bodies reveal the truth about how we honestly feel. If you feel confident, your body will reveal it. If you are ignoring your boundaries, your body will send you signals that you are uncomfortable. If you're angry, your body might clench its muscles and cross its arms. In this case, my body was telling me I was sad and afraid and was helping me pay attention to my fear. Our body and mind are deeply interwoven.[1] Knowing how to weave our body's voice into our lives can help us live more powerfully.

I left my flamenco class ready to listen to the wisdom of my body. I grabbed a Kleenex box and allowed my grief and fears to float to the surface. My body and I were soon dancing in tandem with each other.

In this chapter I will show you several ways to live in tandem with your body. The first step is learning the language of your body. For example, does your body become tense when you are with somebody that is critical and harsh? Perhaps you cross your arms when you don't feel you're being heard. Those physical expressions are your body's way of communicating to you. Knowing how to pay attention to these cues can help you tap into your inner thoughts, needs and feelings.

As you become more acquainted with the language of your body, you can use these physical cues to create more awareness of feelings and thoughts that might otherwise go unnoticed. When your values don't line up with your decisions, your body will let you know. Understanding how your body communicates will empower you to give words to the things that matter to you, set better boundaries, and make decisions that are aligned with your values and needs.

Another way to live in tandem with your body is knowing how to use the mind-body connection to feel more powerful. One way to do that is with a power pose. **Striking a power pose is the practice of standing or sitting in an open or expansive stance in order to increase the feeling of confidence.** Knowing how to shift your body posture to exude more power and self-assurance is a great hack to have for those moments when you need an edge in conversations.

Another great way to live in tandem with your body is

knowing when to sit still or rest. It's a powerful way to listen to what is going on inside of you. I will show you why being still can be just as powerful as moving into action. In this chapter, I will reveal all these insights and more so that you can tap into the powerful wisdom of your body's voice.

## YOUR BODY HAS A VOICE

Throughout this book, I have revealed many habits that can help you own your voice and use it. These habits have included things like lowering any tolerance for crap, learning how to make a good ruckus, and taking up space with your presence. Many of these habits focus on becoming aware of your thoughts and behaviors. Next, I want to show you how your body works in tandem with your voice and how to use your body to connect with your inner voice. I call this the habit of listening to your body's voice.

The more clarity you have, the more you will be able to put your thoughts into action. However, sometimes ambiguity sets in, making it harder to articulate what you think, or need. Even worse, there are probably occasions when you have clarity on your perspective but ignore and dismiss it. We've all been there. Sometimes we just don't listen to our voice. When this happens, your body can be quite good at speaking up for your needs. **Your body is designed to help you listen to your voice.** The first step is to learn the language of your body. It's kind of like this: If you live in Mexico, the more you understand and speak Spanish, the more successful you will be living in there. Similarly, understanding and interpreting the language of your body will help you listen to your voice and live in tandem with your body.

So, what does the language of your body sound like? How does it speak to you? Here's what the language of your body might sound like:

- A tension headache and stomach pain can mean you need to protect yourself from somebody who is making you feel uncomfortable.
- You become physically exhausted after being manipulated into managing somebody's crises. The exhaustion is your body telling you to set better boundaries.
- Your neck feels encircled by a hundred rubber-bands after getting in an argument with someone close to you. That's your body telling you that you need a break from the tension.
- When you haven't had enough time alone, your brain shuts down. You can no longer talk to others without feeling irritable. Your brain is telling you to power down and limit human interaction.
- Your heart races and your fingers fidget when you talk to an emotionally abusive family member. Your body is reflecting your inner tension and telling you to protect yourself.
- You lose your appetite when you feel lonely and sad. Your body is expressing your inner pain.
- You clench your jaw when you say yes when you really want to say no.

Do any of these physical feelings sound familiar to you? Our bodies speak to each of us differently. The more you learn the language of your body, the more equipped you will be to give voice to your needs and perspective. **Our bodies are really good at expressing things that we might not be paying attention to—but should be**. That's because your body has an innate desire to protect you. There are a number of ways it does this.

Most of us can recall times when our gut was telling us to move away from a dangerous situation and then we found out later our instincts were correct. If you've ever had to trust your gut instincts, you were also listening to the protective nature built into your body. Trust the protective nature of your body. These instincts can help alert you to danger.

Your body's protective instincts serve another important function—to protect you relationally and emotionally. It will tell you when you need better boundaries.

Here's how your body's protective instinct might send physical cues when you need better boundaries:

- Your body runs out of energy when you're not getting enough rest (physical boundaries).
- You get a lump in your throat when you say yes to something you don't want to do (personal boundaries).
- Your body is frequently sick from living in a stressful environment (environmental boundaries).
- You feel nauseated and anxious when interacting with a toxic individual (relational boundaries).

That's your body's protective nature speaking up. **These physical reactions are your body's voice talking to you.** I work with a lot of women who have simply stopped listening to their bodies' voices. They have turned the volume down so low they can't hear it. As a result, they feel helpless, unheard, and taken advantage of. However, their bodies' voices never stop talking. If you're not already doing so, learn how to use your body to know when to set boundaries, protect yourself and identify your needs. There are many times when it is reacting to your environment and decisions. Live in tandem with your body by paying attention to its physical cues. This will empower you to set better boundaries and respond to your needs.

*A Coaching Moment:*
*Have a Conversation*
*With Your Body's Voice*

The next time you are in distress, take note of what happens in your body. Then, ask yourself three questions:

1. What am I feeling in my body?

2. As I listen to my body's voice, what is it telling me about my situation?

3. How do I need to respond to what my body is telling me?

Simply observe the signals your body is sending you and

respond. Do you need more self-care? Do you need to say no to something? What do you need to say in order to be heard?

When you first begin to practice this body awareness you might have big insights into your needs. Or you might simply gain a little bit more familiarity with how stress shows up physically. Either way, it's an important step towards learning how to listen to the language of your body.

Your body works in tandem with your voice. Get into the habit of learning its language. It's a powerful way to gain clarity and insight. Then, use this awareness to align your decisions with your values and needs.

## YOUR BODY'S VOICE CAN HELP YOU ALIGN YOUR CHOICES WITH YOUR VALUES AND NEEDS

Over the past thirty years as a psychotherapist, I've had the privilege of working with many wonderful clients. There are times when I notice my clients are in complete denial about their situation. Denial can set in when we are not ready to look at the pain surrounding our specific circumstances. However, sometimes we deny or ignore what feel because we are simply not paying attention to our needs. When I notice my clients doing this, I have them tap into what they are experiencing in their bodies. One of my favorite books, the Bible, says, "Our bodies are fearfully and wonderfully made."[2] This is so true. Our body has a voice filled with wisdom. Tapping into this wisdom enables us to live in tandem with our values and needs.

**Your body is not very good at denial, so when you make**

**a decision that is out of alignment with your values and needs, your body will tell you**. In other words, your body won't ignore the truth about your circumstances. Instead, it will often send you physical symptoms indicating that you need to pay attention to something harmful in your life, like a smoke alarm system in your house. When your body sends a signal, don't ignore it. Instead, look for the smoke and put out the fire.

For example, your stomach might become tight and upset when you're feeling overwhelmed. If so, ask yourself, "What do I need?" Have you noticed you get a tension headache when your needs are ignored? That's your body telling you that's not okay. Have you ever noticed you bite your lip and clench your jaw when you say yes to visiting an overbearing, critical relative? Pay attention to these physical cues. Your body is revealing how you really feel. It does this to help you pay attention to your boundaries and needs. Learn how to listen to the physical cues in your body so you can make changes when necessary.

In the same way that your body tells you something needs to change, it will also tell you when your choices are aligned with your inner voice. For example, you might feel calm and relaxed when your needs are met. Your energy will increase when you implement boundaries. The tension headache will disappear when you say no to toxic situations. Your body communicates to you all day long about whether you are living an authentic life that is aligned with your values and beliefs. **Get into the habit of listening to your body's voice so you can make the choices that are best for you.**

I had a client named Kelsey (not her real name) who had

just discovered her brother-in-law had an affair. Understandably, my client was livid with him and felt protective of her sister, whom he betrayed. She was asked by her family to ignore the affair and politely attend the traditional Christmas family dinner. I asked Kelsey how she felt about going to the family gathering.

Kelsey said, "Well, if my sister is okay with it then I will just have to deal with it. So, I guess I'm fine going to dinner tonight."

I asked Kelsey to briefly scan her body and see what she noticed. She realized her arms were crossed, she was clenching her teeth, biting her lip and the tone of her voice was high pitched. I asked her to close her eyes, take a few deep breaths and take a moment to get in touch with her body. As Kelsey sat quietly and engaged with her breath, she awakened to her senses. I asked Kelsey to notice how her body was feeling. She began to notice her stomach was tight, there was tension in her neck, and her fingers were twitching. She remarked there was a weird pulse in her heart space.

With this awareness in mind, I asked her, "What is your body telling you regarding how you feel about going to dinner with your brother-in-law who cheated on your sister?"

She immediately blurted, "I really do not want to go! I am so angry at him. I can't believe my family is ignoring what happened and not confronting him. In fact, I don't want to see him again until I confront him!" My client sat still for a few minutes as she took in the wisdom of her body. She immediately made the decision to listen to her voice and not attend the dinner. She also told her family why she did not want to go.

Listening to her body helped give Kelsey permission to be less submissive and more proactive with her decision. She stopped ignoring her boundaries. It was a powerful moment for Kelsey. Learning how to listen to her body helped Kelsey find her voice and align her decisions with her values.

Your body has tremendous wisdom. When you're about to make a decision, pause and do a body check. Notice what it is telling you about how to best make the decision. When you feel physical tension, ask yourself if anything is out of alignment in your life. Respect the boundaries your body is communicating to you. These are just a few ways to tap into the language of your body and live in tandem with your values and beliefs.

## HOW TO USE THE MIND-BODY CONNECTION TO FEEL MORE CONFIDENT

As I mentioned earlier, we hold tremendous wisdom in our bodies. So far we have covered how the habit of letting your body speak to you can help you tap into your inner voice. And how to use the language of your body to pay better attention to the things that matter to you. Next, we will explore how to use this mind-body connection to change the way you feel.

Our emotions can impact our bodies. For example, when we are stressed (emotion) we are likely to feel muscle tension (the impact on the body). The reverse is true as well. **You can use your body to impact how you feel**. One way to use this mind-body connection to your advantage is by using a power pose to feel more confident. It's a great way to live in tandem with your body.

**A power pose uses the practice of standing or sitting in an open or expansive stance to increase the feeling of confidence**. I first learned about the concept of a power pose from Amy Cuddy's research on the psychological impact of body language.[3] Cuddy's research showed that when we feel powerless, we make ourselves small and move into "low power" poses; we cross our legs, lower our gaze, lower our heads, and pull our body inward. In contrast, Cuddy's research revealed that "adopting expansive poses increases people's feelings of power and confidence. In other words, when we take up space with our body—spread our arms wide, stand tall, rest our hands on our hips, and raise our chest higher—we feel more powerful. When your body leads, your mind will follow.

I was amazed when I learned her research revealed that a power pose increases levels of testosterone (the hormone linked to power and dominance) and decreases the stress hormone cortisol.[4] In other words, this powerful body language can change our brain chemistry and increase our confidence levels immediately. Knowing a few power poses can help you feel confident fast—before and during important conversations.

Before I speak in front of an audience, hop on a podcast, or step into a coaching session with a high-powered executive, I always practice a few power poses beforehand for at least two minutes. The poses activate my inner strength, boost my confidence immediately, and help me feel powerful.

Let me teach you two of my favorite power poses: Wonder Woman and Victory Woman.

*A Coaching Moment:*
*Boost Your Confidence Quickly*
*with Power Poses*

**Wonder Woman Power Pose**

You might be familiar with this pose if you've watched a Wonder Woman television show or movie. I remember watching Wonder Woman as a young girl and loving how this warrior goddess kicked butt, deflected bullets, and overcame evil. Here's how to do the Wonder Woman power pose:

1. Stand tall with your feet hip-distance apart and planted on the ground.

2. Place your hands on your hips, raise your chest high, and keep your gaze forward.

3. Hold this position for at least two minutes and notice how you feel more ready to take up space and own your power.

**Victory Woman Power Pose**

When an athlete scores a goal or wins a race and then raises her arms in victory, she strikes the Victory Woman power pose. Nobody tells the athlete to move into this pose; she simply does it because in the moment she feels powerful. Here's how to do the Victory Woman power pose:

1. Firmly plant your feet on the ground.

2. Lift your chest and head and lengthen your neck.

3. Lift both your arms toward the sky in a V-shape.

4. Hold this pose for at least two minutes and notice how it feels to inhabit a victorious posture.

I always advise my clients to engage in a power pose before they speak publicly, teach, ask for a raise, or before any other moment when they need to own their value. My clients are amazed by how quickly they feel more courageous. Try a power pose the next time you have a high-pressure situation; invite your body into the process of being more empowered.

## DO NOTHING TO ACCOMPLISH SOMETHING GREAT

Earlier I told a story about being in flamenco class and breaking into tears the minute I settled into a child's pose, a yoga movement designed to rest the body in between moves. As I sank into this restful position, tears ran down my face. **It was in a moment of non-doing that I was finally able to notice what was going on inside me.** It was by doing nothing that I was able to accomplish something important: to tap into my feelings and needs. Sometimes doing nothing, slowing down, and easing away from a hectic schedule can help us accomplish something great.

Throughout this book, you have been challenged to do some hard stuff. Things like pursuing bigger challenges, building bigger platforms, speaking up, stepping into leadership, and taking up space with your perspective and body language. Most of these habits require moving into action. The habit of doing nothing or doing less can be powerful, too. It can help you reconnect with yourself, listen to your voice, listen to your body, and take better care of yourself.

Don't forget to be still and slow down. Don't forget to schedule times in your super busy calendar to do nothing. Use this time to connect with your thoughts and feelings more easily. Find ways to slow down and reflect: turn off your phone for a few hours, go on a walk, journal, meditate, take a stroll in the forest, lie in child's pose, do anything that helps you slow down and check in with yourself. You matter.

During these moments of slowing down, use these coaching questions to check in with yourself:

- How am I feeling?
- What do I need?
- What can I let go of?
- What am I feeling in my body?
- What am I thankful for?
- What do I want next in my life?

Slowing down and being still can help you partner with

your body and check in with yourself. Slowing down long enough to listen to your inner world can lead to a deeper awareness of what needs to happen next in your life.

You have access to the wisdom of your body at any given moment. Become a student of the special ways your body communicates with you. Listen to the cues in your body and use this awareness to make sure you're aligned with your needs and values. Increase your confidence and presence with a power pose. Take the time to be still and listen to your inner voice. All of these habits will empower you to live in tandem with your body and your voice.

## CHAPTER 8 IN A NUTSHELL

1. The habit of listening to your body's voice is a pattern of living in tandem with your body.

2. Your body is designed to help you listen to your inner voice. It will often send you physical cues indicating you need to pay attention to something in your life, kind of like an alarm system that goes off when there's smoke in the house. Listening to these cues can help you determine if you need to change something.

3. Your body is not very good at denial, so when you make a decision that is out of alignment with your values and beliefs, your body will tell you. Your body won't ignore the truth

about your circumstances. It's designed to tell you what you need, how you feel about others, when boundaries are being ignored, and when you need to be more self-protective.

4. A power pose is a great way to tap into the wisdom of our body. Practice a power pose by standing or sitting in an open or expansive stance to increase your feeling of confidence. Power poses quickly change one's self-perception and inner attitude. They work because the body influences the mind. The Wonder Woman and Victory Woman are two power poses that can be used when you need a boost of confidence and want to exude power.

5. Sometimes we need to slow down and be still so we can listen to our inner voice. It's also a great way to check in with yourself and engage in self-care.

## QUESTIONS FOR GROUP OR SELF-REFLECTION

1. What physical signals do you receive from your body when somebody has crossed your boundaries?
2. Think about a time when you did not listen to your body's voice. What happened as a result?
3. Think about a time when you listened to your body. How did you respond and what was the result?
4. What physical signals do you receive from your

body when you are not in alignment with your values and beliefs?

5. If you were to have a conversation with your body at this moment what would the dialogue sound like?

6. When was the last time you slowed down long enough to listen to your inner thoughts?

# EPILOGUE

I am totally indifferent about sports. I typically find out who is playing in the Super Bowl about five minutes before game time. I am much more of a creative-arts kind of gal. However, I do marvel at the expressions used to inspire athletes to give it their all. One of those expressions is "Leave it all on the floor (or field)." It means "Hold nothing back. Give it your all. Win or lose—put all of yourself into the game."

I want to share those same words with you, but from a slightly different and more imaginative angle and for a cause that is more worthy than winning a game—you! In your life, use everything inside of you to turn up the volume on your voice until you are heard and are changing the things that matter to you. Don't hold back. Empty yourself for this cause, knowing that your voice matters. Give it your all! Give this cause everything inside of you because amplifying your voice, your values, your perspective, and who you are at your core is an awe-inspiring mission.

Your hard work will be worth it, I promise. I have seen it in my own life and in the lives of my clients. There will be a moment in this journey where it will all come together. In this sudden, magical moment you will bear the fruits of your hard work.

Build these habits into your daily life, and you will be powerful.

- Embrace the gift of vulnerability so others can witness how amazing you are.
- Take risks so you can experience the thrill of realizing you are more capable than you ever imagined.
- Take up space with your presence so that the world will know you are a force to be reckoned with.
- Assert your voice so that you can move your beliefs into action.
- Lower your tolerance for crap because you are worthy of protecting.
- Create meaningful tension when you need to champion your values and perspective.
- Listen to your body's voice so you can compassionately attend to your needs.
- Embody your inner chingona like your life depends on it. She will remind you to unapologetically own who you are.

Go get 'em, ladies. And when you do, remember that I am with you on your journey, encouraging you every step of the way, cheering you on while drinking my gin and tonic and imagining how life will change because you dared to have a bigger voice in the world!

Bendición,

Margo

# GLOSSARY

**Authenticity.** Being your true self and making sure who you are on the inside matches who you are on the outside.

**Boundary.** A line that marks what is and is not okay with you. Boundaries are the limits you create that determine how others behave towards you and how you respond to others when they pass those limits.

**Chingona.** (Spanish) A woman who follows her own path. She is fierce, independent, tough, and confident. She is not afraid to speak her mind and make her voice heard; she is empowered and seeks her own approval. Historically, this is a derogatory term used to refer to a woman who is assertive or bossy.

**Codependency.** A pattern of meeting the needs and expectations of others in order to feel loved and valued. It usually involves tolerating crap that should not be tolerated.

**Commanding posture.** Taking control of your body language during critical conversations and making sure it conveys confidence and authority.

**Diplomatic assertiveness.** A method of communicating that uses the skills of tact and conciliation combined with a firm and clear point of view.

**Duende.** (Spanish) A word used in flamenco dancing to refer to an authentic and confident expression of who you are that is inspiring to others.

**Emotional habits.** A pattern of thoughts and behaviors on autopilot. Emotional habits influence how we make decisions and how we view ourselves. They lay the foundation for a lot of what happens in our lives.

**Good enough equation.** A mindset that allows you to set aside any belief that says you need to achieve your goals perfectly and instead gives you permission to be "good enough. A "good enough" mindset almost always outperforms an "I need to do it perfectly" mindset.

**Imposter syndrome.** The feeling of being in a place you don't belong because you don't feel good enough—even though you are.

**Inner resource.** A preexisting strength that surfaces during demanding, stressful, or challenging moments.

**Living an empowered life.** Having the ability to influence the things that matter most to you because you can set aside anything that keeps you from making healthy decisions for yourself.

**Meaningful tension.** When conflict is created in order to protect something you value or create necessary change.

**Mission mantra.** A simple statement you can say to yourself when you feel stuck, discouraged, or unmotivated to pursue your goal.

**Own your story.** When you own your story, you recognize how your past has shaped your views and self-perception, and you quiet any shame that might keep you from being vulnerable. Part of this process includes redefining the difficult moments in your life by giving them meaning and purpose.

**People-pleasing.** The habit of perpetually responding to the wishes, expectations, or demands of others, while neglecting your own.

**Perfectionism.** A tendency to set personal standards that are so high they either cannot be met, or they can only be met with great difficulty. It also includes a tendency to see even minor imperfections in oneself as unacceptable or horrible.

**Platform.** Any medium that enables you to be seen or heard.

**Power pose.** The practice of standing or sitting in an open or expansive stance in order to increase one's feeling of confidence.

**Self-awareness.** Having an accurate and honest understanding of who you are.

**Shame.** The feeling that you are less than others, that you are not good enough, or that there is something wrong with you.

**Show up as yourself.** To truly be who you are as a person and not an image of somebody you think you should be; to make sure your thoughts, words, and actions are an honest representation of who you are.

**Taking up space.** To use your perspective, body language, and voice to claim a position of leadership and authority.

**Visibility.** The act of intentionally being seen and heard. Visibility means finding ways to promote your leadership style, ideas, and perspective.

**Vision statement**. A descriptive statement that reflects why you want to pursue a specific goal.

**Voice**. The authentic expression of your values, perspective, and who you are at the core.

**Vulnerability.** The courage to fully reveal who you are.

# ACKNOWLEDGMENTS

This book took me twenty years to write, even though I've only been putting words on the page for the last three years. In those twenty years, I encountered all of the people who have made this book possible. I would like to thank some of them here.

I would first like to thank Tabby Biddle, my mentor, coach, friend and inspiration-extraordinaire! I would still be standing in the shadows were it not for your great leadership and love. I will forever be grateful for your wisdom, support, and the example you set for all women. You have changed the course of my life forever.

I would like to thank Camila Furr-Marquez, my late-night-walking, sequence-playing, cocktail-making, fellow INFP. You read my book not once, but twice!! That is true love! You were with me from the very beginning of this marathon and ran across the finish line with me, standing by my side as I sent in the final manuscript. I am so grateful for your support and the wisdom you provided for this book. More than that, I am thankful you are in my life. Gracias!

Shawna Burkhart, you are more than a friend. You are my sister from another mother. Thank you for the many "power hours" that kept me focused on this mission. You've picked me up off the floor and bandaged my aching ego more than once. Thank you for all the ways you've looked after my soul. Your middle name should be "unconditional love." Thank you for reading my book, for your brilliant insights, for your kind words, and for reassuring me that my book didn't suck. I adore you and can't imagine life without you.

Lisa Ayres, thank you for generously providing space at Lincoln Way Inn where I could hunker down in silence to reflect and write. Thank you for reading my book and for the insights that improved this book immensely. I adore your wild-hearted soul and am inspired every single moment I am in your company. Thank you for sprinkling your magic pixie dust on this book and in my life.

Katie Rose Guest Pryal, my editor and book-champion: you are a word-goddess! You inspire me, encourage me, and intimidate the hell out of me. You are a chingona, through and through. You are exactly what I needed. You courageously jumped into a raft with me and said "yes" to a white-water ride. You challenged me and pushed hard— because you wanted me to see I was more capable than I realized. Thank you, Sensei. Somehow, you managed to make an author out of me. I am infinitely grateful for your brilliance. This book would be in the shredder if it weren't for the "Katie Touch." Thank you. I am eternally grateful.

Lauren Faulkenberry, my copyeditor, book publishing coach, cover designer, and cheerleader. You gently scraped me off the ground after a few meltdowns with encouraging words of wisdom. You have a remarkable ability to hold sacred space for others. You are a saint and one of the kindest women I have ever met. I will forever be grateful for the immense role you have played in helping me launch this book. Thank you.

Anna Marquez-Perez, my goddaughter and fellow fashionista! Thank you for continually asking how my writing was coming along, for listening to my book content, and for your invaluable feedback regarding how to write my personal story. Our "nine-hour conversation marathons" provided endless inspiration for this book and my life. I absolutely adore you!

To all of my nieces, I hope this book helps pave the way for you, your children, and the next generation of kick-ass Latinas!

Wendy Clinard, my flamenco teacher: thank you for all of the dance wisdom you instilled into my life and soul. You didn't just provide dance lessons. You provided life lessons that left me with many of the "a-ha" moments I have written about in this book.

Dori Krasnopolsky, thank you for your boundless support —both in my life and with this book. I am in awe of how a Wheaton College sweatshirt and a serendipitous moment in a park lead to a twenty-five-year friendship. Thank you for being "my person".

To my clients, I have learned so much from each of you. Thank you for trusting me with your stories and inviting me into your lives. I have learned so much from your strength, tenacity, and courage.

I am thankful to God, whose amazing grace redeemed my story and my life.

Thank you to all my friends and family who continually asked how my book was coming along. And kept asking.

And kept asking. This book took FOREVER, but you hung in there and reminded me that I had something worth saying. I am so thankful for the encouragement each of your interactions provided. It takes a village.

Mamasita, aka, "pioneer woman": You are the strongest woman I know. Thank you for modeling strength, tenacity, faith, gentleness, and dependable love. I hope I can pass down your wisdom to the next generation. My book was inspired by your story. I love you more!!!!

Dad, thank you for showing me how to work hard, be the boss, and be an entrepreneur. You're still the best! We miss you.

To my sisters, Bertha Costales and Rosie Artuso: I am sustained by your endless supply of love, support, infinite prayers, and green chilé.

To my grandmothers, who paved the way for a legion of strong chingona women: your legacies live on.

Grandpa, I still miss you every single day, but I can feel your presence whenever I am with my fierce, God-loving aunts. When I need to remember what really matters in life, I run home to them. Your unconditional love and stability set the foundation for my strength. I hope you can read my book in heaven.

Francisco, my son: I adore you, your determination, your grit, and your strength. Your voice flows with the confidence of a man who knows who he is. You are paving the way to make the world a better place for the LGBTQ community, and I am so proud of the good you have accomplished. Continue to use your powers for good. Thank you for always believing in me. I miss you and I know why. My heart loves yours endlessly.

Marisa, aka, "Jane": my daughter: I love your wild-hearted, chingona, don't-take-nothing-from-nobody spirit. Thank you for sharing your Instagram magic to help spread the word about this book. You bring me immeasurable joy and hope. You are wise beyond your years. I am in awe of the woman you have become. You are using the power of your voice to make life easier for the next BIPOC generation and I could not be prouder of you. You are both, "ruling the world and setting it in on fire!" I love you to the moon and back. Xiomara.

Frank, my husband, you are the love of my life, my soulmate, and the owner of my heart. Any place feels like home when I am with you. Your relentless love and endless support gave me the strength I needed to put my voice out into the world. You made me laugh when I was sad. You picked me up when I was down. You washed the dishes when I was nowhere to be found. I am the woman I am today because of you. Thank you for providing the stories, advice, support, and space I needed to write this book. I could not have done it without you. You are my rock and my steady love.

# NOTES

## 1. THE HABIT OF OWNING YOUR VOICE

1. United States Census Bureau, "Educational Attainment, by Race and Hispanic Origin: 1960 to 1998," in *Statistical Abstract of the United States: 1999*, at 160. Accessed January 29, 2022. https://www.census.gov/prod/99pubs/99statab/sec04.pdf.
2. Ware is quoted in "The Neuroscience of Behavior Change," *StartUp Health*, August 8, 2017. https://healthtransformer.co/the-neuroscience-of-behavior-change-bcb567fa83c1.

## 2. THE HABIT OF TAKING MORE RISKS

1. Tara Sophia Mohr, "Why Women Don't Apply for Jobs Unless They're 100% Qualified," Harvard Business Review, March 2, 2018, https://hbr.org/2014/08/why-women-dont-apply-for-jobs-unless-theyre-100-qualified.
2. Watty Piper, *The Little Engine That Could* (Grosset & Dunlap 2001; orig. Platt & Munk 1930).

## 3. THE HABIT OF LOWERING YOUR TOLERANCE FOR CRAP

1. Melody Beattie, *Codependent No More: How to Stop Controlling Others and Start Caring for Yourself* (Hazelden 1986).
2. If you want to take a deeper dive into the anatomy of boundaries, I highly recommend reading the following two books. Nedra Glover Tawwab, *Set Boundaries, Find Peace: A Guide to Reclaiming Yourself* (Tarcher Perigree 2021); Anne Katherine, *Where to Draw the Line: How to Set Healthy Boundaries Every Day* (Fireside 2000).

# 4. THE HABIT OF EMBRACING YOUR INNER CHINGONA

1. "Muy Chingona," *Urban Dictionary*, Accessed January 12, 2021. https://www.urbandictionary.com/define.php?term=Muy=Chingona.
2. "New Study: Women Judged More Harshly When Speaking up Assertively," *Yahoo! Finance*, August 5, 2015. https://finance.yahoo.com/news/study-women-judged-more-harshly-120000656.html.
3. *Kieran Snyder*, "The Abrasiveness Trap: High Achieving Men and Women are Described Differently in Reviews," *Fortune.com*, August 26, 2014. https://fortune.com/2014/08/26/performance-review-gender-bias/.
4. [4] Ellie Lisitsa, "How to Fight Smarter: Soften Your Start-Up," *The Gottman Institute*, not dated, accessed March 9, 2022, https://www.gottman.com/blog/softening-startup.

# 5. THE HABIT OF VULNERABILITY

1. Brené Brown, "The Power of Vulnerability," TEDxHouston, June 2010, TED.com. https://www.ted.com/talks/brene_brown_the_power_of_vulnerability.
2. Brown, "The Power of Vulnerability."
3. Brené Brown, "Shame vs. Guilt," brenebrown.com, Jan. 15, 2013, https://brenebrown.com/articles/2013/01/15/shame-v-guilt/.
4. Brené Brown, "Listening to Shame," TED2012, March 2012, TED.com. https://www.ted.com/talks/brene_brown_listening_to_shame.

# 6. THE HABIT OF TAKING UP SPACE

1. ScienceDaily, "Body Posture Affects Confidence in Your Own Thoughts, Study Finds," ScienceDaily.com, Oct. 5, 2009. https://www.sciencedaily.com/releases/2009/10/091005111627.htm.
2. Amy Cuddy, "Your Body Language May Shape Who You Are." TEDGlobal 2012, June 2012, TED.com. https://www.ted.com/talks/amy_cuddy_your_body_language_shapes_who_you_are.
3. David Gilmour, "Emma González Now Has More Twitter Followers than the NRA," *The Daily Dot*, Feb. 26, 2018. https://www.dailydot.-

com/debug/emma-gonzaleztwitter-followers-nra/.

4.  Marley Dias, #1000BlackGirlBooks, accessed March 9, 2022, https://www.marleydias.com/1000blackgirlbooks.

5.  Amanda Berlin (www.amandaberlin.com) offers online classes, group coaching, and one-on-one support for women who want to get clear on their message and build bigger platforms. Amy Porterfield (https://www.amyporterfield.com) is an online marketing guru who offers numerous online opportunities to help build an online presence. Take the Lead (www.taketheleadwomen.com) propels all women of all diversities towards their fair share of leadership, by offering workshops, coaching and conferences.

## 7. THE HABIT OF KNOWING WHO YOU ARE

1.  Dan Cassidy, "10 Things Successful People Do to Achieve Greatness," *Lifehack.org*, not dated, last accessed March 9, 2022. https://www.life-hack.org/articles/communication/10-things-successful-people.html.

2.  Malala Yousafzai, "Malala's Story," Malala Fund, Malala.org, accessed March 1, 2022. https://malala.org/malalas-story.

## 8. THE HABIT OF LISTENING TO YOUR BODY'S VOICE

1.  Helen Payne, "Our Body and Mind Are One," *LINK*, 1(1), 2014. https://www.herts.ac.uk/link/volume-1-issue-1/our-body-and-mind-are-one.

2.  *Psalms* 139:14-24, Bible, New International Version.

3.  David Biello, "Inside the Debate about Power Posing: A Q&A with Amy Cuddy." IDEAS.TED.COM, Feb. 22, 2017. https://ideas.t-ed.com/inside-the-debate-about-power-posing-a-q-a-with-amy-cuddy/.

4.  Dana R. Carney, Amy J. C. Cuddy, and Andy J. Yap, "Power Posing: Brief Nonverbal Displays Affect Neuroendocrine Levels and Risk Tolerance," *Psychological Science*, 21(10): 1363-38, 2010. DOI: 10.1177/0956797610383437.

## ABOUT THE AUTHOR

Margo Tirado MA, LCPC is a psychotherapist, life coach, speaker and story-teller. She received her degree in Clinical Psychology from Wheaton College and owns a private practice in Hinsdale, Illinois. For over two decades, Margo has studied the emotional habits that empower women to possess self-confidence, influence and power. Her insights have been shared at a TEDx talk at Grant Park Chicago, on the radio and in numerous retreats, podcasts, webinars and women's conferences. She is the co-creator of the DASH Conference for women, a unique one-day conference that helps women build stronger emotional habits. She has been invited to speak at faith-based organizations to share her thoughts about the absence of women in leadership and how to close that gap. She helped launch The Center for Women in Leadership, a grass roots program focused on developing feminine leadership in church circles. She uses insights from over 40,000 hours of clinical experience, as well as her personal story, to teach women how to stand tall and have a bigger voice in the world.

Margo, originally from New Mexico, is married to her best friend Frank and has raised two amazing adults, Francisco and Marisa. For fun, she dances flamenco, loves entertaining and is often found in her kitchen where she is known for serving friends eight-course meals when they come to dinner!

Visit her website at margotirado.com and view her TEDx talk at bit.ly/margotedx.

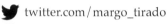 twitter.com/margo_tirado
 instagram.com/margotirado
linkedin.com/in/margo-tirado

## WORK WITH MARGO

Do you want to have a bigger voice in the world, but need help to make that happen? Take the next step and continue your work with Margo.

Reach out to schedule your complimentary consultation and learn more about Margo's 10-week one-on-one private coaching program for women who are ready for empowerment.

Visit her at **margotirado.com**

### Margo Tirado
Empowering Women

Made in the USA
Coppell, TX
13 March 2023